ULTRATHOUGHTS™ TRIPARTITE

GODHEAD DESIGNS

THE EVOLUTION OF SACRED IDEAS AND PHILOSOPHY IN BRIEF

W. DURWOOD JOHNSON

Publisher: Ultrathoughts™ LLC
ultrathoughtsbook@gmail.com
www.ultrathoughts.com

Godhead Designs: The Evolution of Sacred Ideas and Philosophy in Brief

ISBN: 978-1-951731-02-1 (Print)
ISBN: 978-1-951731-03-8 (Ebook)
Library of Congress Control Number: 2019917078

Cover Design by Berge Design

CONTENTS

PART IV

INSPIRATIONS

Special thanks to few great poetic authors.

Robert Barclay

Martin Luther

Origen

Marcus Aurelius

Plato

Thomas Aquinas

Rene' Descartes

John Locke

PREFACE

Ideology is an interesting facet of the mind. It guides a unique truth while often denying its own existence. It is reflected in your automatic response to a serious question. Ideology is the body of myth, belief, and doctrine that guides future judgement.

My sisters definitely have opinions rooted in fundamental ideology. In both their views I am a bit strange. "Obsessive" was the word one of them used. They noticed my obsessive personality well before I did. Siblings provide valuable feedback. Perhaps I should have paid more attention to them. Had I learned at an early age to restrain my obsessive nature, maybe I would be relaxing on a beach somewhere instead of obsessing about completing this manuscript. After all, I am not a professional writer—just a person who thinks way too much.

Since siblings provide valuable feedback, I have some for my sisters. One is obviously an extremely rational thinker, the other a classic example of an imaginative thinker. Each is intelligent, educated, and engaging. Still, they have very different ways of looking at things; very different ideologies. If asked to explain why she supports one notion over another, each could rattle off facts, examples, and probably even provide quotes from scholarly research in support of her position, but neither truly understands why she tends to think as she does.

There is a reason we each have a truth and its creator is the mind. Over time your mind writes and rewrites a type of narrative within. The mind is influenced in its writing by the brain, which is fundamentally a product of an individual's DNA. DNA imprints a tendency, a fundamental ideological leaning to think more from the logical-left or creative-right hemisphere of the brain. The tendency has a continual influence on the story of mind as we mature. Though our mind creates our reality, we can say our fundamental ideology begins as a result of biology.

This innate leaning becomes more pronounced with time unless efforts are taken to stop the inclination. For many, their orientation and fundamental outlook will eventually overwhelm fair-minded discernment. Of course, in order to correct a flaw one must first admit the problem. This brings me back to the unfortunate fact that bias is generally denied by its owner. Ideological viewpoint is so basic to our person that our bias is simply who we are—how we think. To alter something so foundational is very difficult and though it may never be absolutely overcome, a bias tendency can be suppressed when appreciated. Your personal mind-myth narrative can be altered enough to reconsider your truth and ultimately your reality through intentional thought.

I have awareness of my leaning toward the logical-left brain hemisphere and an appreciation of my obsessive tendencies. I've had some success in restraining my overly rational disposition but have yet to figure out how to restrain my obsessive nature. This has led me to undertake the nearly overwhelming task of writing a trilogy as my very first work.

With an understanding that my views are fundamentally skewed and inherently flawed, I fight every day to balance my mind. The goal of my constant attempts to get the balance right is to limit the influence my innate leaning has on my version of the world and truth itself. I do so because I believe I can be a better person tomorrow than today if I step outside of my reflexive thinking. Since my sisters fail to appreciate their own bias, they don't have any interest in limiting its impact. Each has matured to perceive the other as naïve, misled, or even menacing on occasion. Over time, this has led to their reluctance to interact in meaningful ways.

This is a shame, but not uncommon. People tend to get and stay immersed within an ideology that clouds their view. Any view other than their own is therefore wrong. The only question that remains is an evaluation of whether the error is intentional or not.

Such a way of thinking often leads to conflict when my sisters choose to interact. As they mature, what were once relatively minor differences of opinion grow tiresome. A simple annoyance eventually becomes a frustrating situation. Anger and ultimately antipathy toward one another will soon be the result. I've seen it in others. I assume you have as well. In fact, this dynamic is playing out in our current political, social, and economic environment.

When we don't communicate, we eventually drop any pretense of appreciation for one another. Such loss of respect means we forfeit a chance to learn and grow. Our conclusions, truth, and world views become even more distorted and fundamentally skewed. In our world today, more of our friends are choosing to divide and ignore. I'm fearful of where society is headed.

In my family, I have always been the mediator. I have a knack for getting between two sisters and promoting common ground. This is not something I have always enjoyed, but it is something I am quite good at. I am a mediator at heart. This second book of three is a continuation of my attempt to foster more respectful communication among us all and promote the exchange of ideas.

INTRODUCTION

The title of this series of three short books is collectively called the Ultrathoughts Tripartite, a wordplay on a concept developed by Plato. He was the ultimate promoter of the idea that thinking itself is important for humanity. A favorite idea of his was that three separate parts can each act in their own best interest without interfering with one another. The three parts exist separately, but in cooperation they present a new and different form, a tripartite. I think of my books that way. They each stand alone, but taken in unison they present my broader idea that human beings are losing what makes them special on this planet. I pay homage to Plato with the series title.

A specific goal of mine is to encourage people to form deep, contemplative thoughts while restraining their ideological bias. I call this process ultra-thinking. When successful, your fair and open mind will urge the brain to engage both hemispheres, the logical-left and the creative-right, in creation of an Ultrathought. This type of active whole-brain ultra-thinking enhances the quality of your self-constructed narrative, your mind-myth, as it seeks to create a more meaningful and well-conceived personal truth. Such a deeply considered truth might be so worthy as to be considered enlightenment. Regardless of whether you confirm your existing beliefs, create fresh new ideas, or experience enlightenment, your more refined conclusions are not only good for you, they are good for humanity. Book one was devoted to a thorough exploration of ideological bias and mind.

Our species is a thinking animal and we have the ability get quite good at thought creation. You are a born thinker who seeks to understand something more. As an ultra-thinker you will elect to explore a more lucid version of truth and write a richer narrative of the mind as you do so. The story of your mind is constantly written with or without your own conscious guidance. A purposeful thinker can write poetry within their own narrative that not only helps the poet; it may in fact stand the test of time and benefit humanity. In this book you will be reminded of some poetic ideas of history. These Ultrathoughts have undoubtedly benefitted millions of people. I urge you to become a poet today and write your narrative with intent. Regardless of the quality of your poetic creation, your own poetry will take flight and become a butterfly within your mind.

This book stands on its own but does expand on ideas of a spiritual realm discussed in the first, *Intentional Thought*. What follows is an extremely brief recap of various Godhead designs offered in chronological succession along with an exploration of the relationship between science and spiritual beliefs. The philosophies discussed are prime examples of the benefits of ultra-thinking. These are Ultrathoughts that have stood the test of time. Are the ideas presented here foolish or brilliant? I've taken one philosophy class in my whole life, and that was only because I needed a liberal arts credit, so if there is a judge of wisdom it's certainly not me. In the series it's unfortunate that from time to time my tone sounds academic; please understand I am just a person who was foolish enough to think he could write a series of books about mind and spirituality in hopes of helping a few people. In fairness to my effort this attempt highlights a hidden nuance of the premise. We need no license, no letters, no PhD to think. A philosopher or any thinking being simply chooses to contemplate, and they alone judge the quality of their thoughts.

Be fearless, respect no arbiter of thoughts. Challenge yourself to contemplate the outrageous.

Ultra-thinking any topic is tough, but in this book we specifically explore the hardest subject of all, the Godhead. It's difficult because the idea is so integral to our personal narrative and for many of us, we've been indoctrinated to believe that to contemplate God is to question God. To question God, as the theory goes, is to jeopardize your very soul for eternity. Make no mistake: personally I don't care if, whether, or how you believe. In my own belief no manifest truth of any God design will ever be proven by me one way or another. In this work I merely suggest ultra-thinking is important, and ultra-thinking the Godhead is a worthy subject for contemplation. Maybe you would rather fearlessly ultra-think economics and personal finance, which is exactly what I do in a soon-to-be-finished fourth book based on the Ultrathoughts concept.

Your ideas about God are intertwined with the person you present, and to ultra-think, you must attempt to think differently than your historical narrative. If you believe in the individual soul or in a type of world soul, contemplation of God is probably considered quite important to you. However, your appreciation of a God doesn't mean you will ever choose to ultra-think the nature of the Godhead. You could believe in God reflexively or out of deference to your society and live a lifetime without ultra-thinking or even deeply contemplating your views. There is nothing inherently wrong with this. However, I suggest we each strive to be more than our reflexive thoughts create. Each of us should be a person of purpose not simply one of ideological leaning. No topic is, therefore, beyond reconsideration.

Of course, you may believe you have no hint of God theory within your mind. In such a case, you may deduce that theories or designs of the Godhead are no different than concepts of the tooth fairy—each an interesting idea but literally irrelevant in practical terms. As a consequence of your impressions you may think that while consideration of God could be fun, it is rather trivial. Respectfully, I disagree. Godhead scrutiny is serious work. Such contemplation touches the core of your personal mind-myth narrative because spiritual belief is innate to our species. If you believe you have no Godhead belief, I suggest that may simply be because you've either unintentionally lost it in the clutter of your narrative or you've successfully de-programmed what is an innate part of being human from your myth.

Spiritual belief can be stricken from a conscious mind. Intelligent adults thinking with lucid minds can elect to deny any hint of God. They are not fools or evil devils when they deny God; they simply don't believe in any Godhead design. Case in point, two of the kindest most moral people I've ever known have described themselves as being atheist. That doesn't mean no thought has ever crossed their minds in regards to the Godhead. It simply means that as a mature adult, each has elected to relegate ideas of the Godhead to a category of fantasy. In doing so, the narrative of the mind classifies spiritual concepts as a fiction having no significant hope of reconsideration absent serious fair-minded contemplation. Such contemplation is not likely but certainly doable.

Interestingly, a naïve child won't deny Godhead belief. Children are reflexively drawn to the idea without fear. I suggest this offers rather obvious proof that thoughts of God are innate. The texture certainly varies, but the general concept is innate in people. With that said, ideas of God must be appreciated to a certain extent to be realized, to be made manifestly important to the person. I am not suggesting God is always denied without awareness. What I am doing is suggesting that denial of mind, whether said denial is intentional or not, removes awareness of a Godhead presence that may or may not actually exist.

My pitch in the series is that we should attempt to think more contemplatively while being fair-minded, rather than think automatically or reflexively. Specifically in this volume I submit that if you dare, you may find it beneficial to contemplate God in the deepest of depths through ultra-thinking.

Godhead contemplation goes to your core and understanding your core is crucial to your best presentation of self within our society. As a result, contemplation of the Godhead may be the single most important task of your life. With enough effort you can rethink and even ultra-think God. If to think is good, then to think the heaviest of topics is the best. To promote my objectives I will present a variety of designs or ideas about the Godhead. This may give you confidence to challenge and, ultimately, strengthen your own Godhead belief. As you'll soon learn, God has been represented many ways depending on the era and location.

Part I

CHAPTER 1

DADDY ISSUES

If you're like most people on the planet, the idea of God is an impression you have considered. Consideration brings an opportunity for refinement. Still, there is no guarantee. It is probable that at least your early attempts to "figure things out" blurred these impressions more than refined them. Certainly, this was my experience from a young age on through my thirties. What I failed to understand is that no idea, concept, or design can be proven a truth. I have come to accept that a relevant reality to a thinking being is that which is thought. To make the statement is no denial of any reality, physical or meta (non-physical); it is simply an acknowledgement that mind creates impressions that dominate my world. We were born to think and my thoughts—delusions or illusions of mind—are my reality.

If you currently harbor a validated Godhead set of beliefs within your mind, you have your God, the superhuman presence that defies physical explanation. Yours may reconcile nicely with millions if not hundreds of millions of others. Possibly you're quite comfortable and settled spiritually. In this book we discuss designs of God as an exploration of ideas. Familiarizing yourself with the views of others may challenge you to ultra-think your own concept, and I believe many people would benefit from such an experience. Obviously, "many" is not all people.

Don't ultra-think the Godhead without pausing to consider both the challenge and the risks involved. If discovering God was easy, our bars and stores wouldn't be full of people seeking solace. Ultra-thinking the Godhead may risk your very soul, and the last thing I want to do is encourage you to take on a journey for which you are not prepared.

With that said, I do suggest that to doubt yourself can strengthen a belief in the end. If you have a weak view of the Godhead, then ultra-thinking your design may be well worth your efforts. If you have never deeply contemplated the spiritual domain of the Godhead, I absolutely believe the effort will be extremely valuable. To think is good for you and humanity. If after daring to think of God in the style of ultra-thinking you refresh your view or validate a new truth altogether, the risk was worth the bet on the blessed power of both God and the human mind.

Assuming I haven't scared or offended you too much, I must get very personal in this chapter. I can't honestly present my interpretation of the Ultrathoughts of the great thinkers of old without disclosing my ideology. I tried to work around it because I don't want you to be left with the impression that I seek to promote my own views. I am no evangelist and would rather pray in a closet than in a church. With that said, I know that though I attempt to suppress my ideology my personal bias tints my words. Without full disclosure I might inadvertently promote my truth of God in a subversive manner. I've decided I'd rather be thought of as a self-indulgent fool for presenting both my journey and my views than a deceiver for not doing so.

Out of pure ignorance I found myself on a quest for God, and for some reason (maybe the spiritual realm itself needs the credit, or blame as it were) I continued to stumble along my own convoluted search-for-God trail for decades. I don't know if I'll ever find the end of the trail, but I'm happily sitting at a rest stop today. Is this stop any better than the place I started? I honestly don't know. Many days I wish I would have never dared to take that first step. Unfortunately, I was such a rube that I only discovered the trail after wandering it for years.

My neighbors, my friends, and my family thought of God in unison. With love and good intentions I was, as a child, instructed that he is a literal superhuman presence with powers who loved me more than any created being. Society told me he is my spiritual father whose importance exceeds any mortal being; in fact, he is the father of us all. This father demanded respect, worship if you will. Therefore, if any individual person denied Father his due, said person would not "sit at the right hand of God" but be subject to an eternity of literal torture after the body has passed. This summarizes what I was told. I can reliably tell you I believed it; partially out of fear but mostly because I really tried not to think of it often. For the first couple decades of my life, I sort of crossed my fingers and hoped for the best. All of this would change as I dared to undertake a journey in exploration of outrageous ideas by others concerning the Godhead. Many of those ideas—ideas by Pythagoras, Plato, Origen, Aquinas, and others—are summarized to the best of my understanding in the following pages.

Whether we recognize it or not every expedition has a starting point, but before any journey we take on baggage. For most of us who end up on the search-for-God trail, that baggage is packed at a very early age. My personal pack was filled to the brim by loving parents and an involved community. I suspect I rarely paid attention to the supply of indoctrination that was supposed to sustain me for an eternity. Unfortunately, I was prepared to visit a literal God along a proven trail but was searching for a spiritual one along a path yet to be cleared.

Early in my childhood I became intrigued by the idea that one day we would witness the end of the world. This shouldn't have been a surprise. After all, I frequently attended a church that promoted a dogma that at any point, possibly before you can read this sentence, God would destroy the planet. Thankfully, my friends and I were assured that we would be spared somehow if we just kept our faith. I wasn't exactly sure about the particulars, but I hoped and prayed I was safe.

About the time I started to incorporate these spiritual beliefs in my mind, sometime before the age of ten, it so happened society became fascinated by a book called *The Late, Great Planet Earth* by Hal Lindsey. The book has sold nearly 30 million copies since its release in 1970 and was extremely popular in certain regions of the country. The book presents a very literal interpretation of the book of Revelations from the Christian Bible. In the spirit of *City of God* by Saint Augustine more than a thousand years before, Lindsey enthralled his audience with his vivid descriptions of the rapture, a time when true Christian believers alone would be saved from the wrath of God and Hell of Satan.

I'm not certain if I read parts of it—that seems unlikely unless it had pictures. However, I definitely knew of Hal Lindsey's take on the biblical story. Bible stories in general fascinated me as a boy. Like so many others I was intrigued by the entire idea of an evil devil facing off against God in an end of the world battle. This drama kept my mind occupied for days. Being left-brain oriented toward logical explanations I couldn't be content with the idea that this could all be simply fantasy from the mind of Lindsey; I needed to make sense of these stories.

At a young age, I was being double-indoctrinated. First by my society, which was influencing me to perceive of God literally, and next by my left-leaning brain, which was constantly reminding me that logic must guide any truth. This dynamic was occurring in the mind of a young boy during a period in history when the United States happened to be obsessed with nuclear war. Looking back today, it seems I jumbled several end-of-world narratives within my very young but deeply rational mind. This combination of a very literal God belief, a book about the wrath of God, and an awareness of a coming nuclear holocaust demanded a reasonable explanation in order to comfortably fit within my budding ideology. That explanation never came.

While that may summarize the beginnings of my obsession with God and the fate of humanity, it was decades later that this common focus of many became a problem for me. Though I was never much of a reader, I happened to pick up a well-illustrated book on the Great Pyramid of Giza. I read it cover to cover. I don't recall the very first of these types of books I read because I read several that were similar. Regardless, I eventually became fascinated by the mysteries surrounding all pyramids. My obsession with pyramids grew and soon morphed into an obsession with Egypt as I continually read any number of books written by Graham Hancock, Robert M. Schoch, and John Anthony West. To give you an idea of my fixation, I went to Egypt in an attempt to figure things out for myself. I proved nothing of course, but I continued to do casual research. My favorite authors are noted if not controversial thinkers who theorize about ancient times in our prehistory. Using a variety of themes, they separately promote the broader idea that civilization is far older than mainstream scientists tell us. With outlines of their ideas in my head, my interest in Egypt further evolved into a fascination with the prehistory of humanity and the specific anthropology of our species. I've never had any formal training in the subjects of anthropology or ancient cultures so my mind should have been a blank slate.

Attempting to explain humanity within the context of my indoctrination about God, I found myself contrasting various versions of the English Bible with Egyptian funerary texts as described by Hancock. What foundation I had about the history of humanity was skewed toward a Judeo-Christian perspective, and the views of my favorite authors definitely didn't mix well with my existing set of beliefs. I needed to reconcile competing facts. Having obtained reproductions of Bibles going back earlier than the year 1600, I checked and rechecked translations seeking to read the true words of God. This led me to specifically contrast Christian writings with various perceptions of the Godhead throughout history.

I then found myself reviewing pure philosophy assuming various historical authors had somehow gleaned truth from the source, God himself. Not understanding my biased nature, of course, I relied upon my left-leaning logical mind to decipher the truth I knew existed. I read dozens of Godhead theories and tried to figure out who had the perfect philosophy. There had to have been an answer discovered by someone. All of the information and the knowledge I accumulated was strictly of a scientific nature. I probably wasn't so much contemplating as I was researching. I had accumulated pages of notes, book outlines, and Wikipedia reprints. I was a detective searching for the truth. I did mention I am no philosopher, didn't I? I am a person who prefers to consider rational topics that produce calculated results. I was doomed to fail in my quest to explain God.

I had spent years trying to prove the unprovable without understanding the nuance of science itself, the difference between the methodology and the non-spiritual religion. I had ultimately fallen for the deception, which is why I pound home the point that the methodology of science cannot accept any concept of the meta in explanation. If from time to time you note my very personal resentment toward certain ideas promoted by scientists, maybe you understand why. The non-spiritual religion of science may be worthy; however, one will never explain any meta or Godhead concept through an application of the methodology. Read my first book if you want more background, but it is a fact that a seeker of the meta is wasting time in using the methodology of science.

My ultimate failure to comprehend the meta or spiritual realm and prove to myself a worthy truth of God made me extremely frustrated. I had believed my mind could literally solve any question given enough effort. Given my obsessive nature, I didn't admit the challenge was bigger than I could ever imagine until I had seemingly wasted years of research and effort. In time I did resolve my mind—the meta mysteries would always remain. God would remain a mystery and I either believed or not. The answer wasn't necessarily comforting, but in a way it did seem to make sense. Now, I needed to reflect.

Why did all of this create such conflict for me? I know I am obsessive, but am I mad? I started to do some serious soul-searching. I was now not seeking God, I was seeking an understanding of my mind and its comprehension of a given truth.

In engaging this new obsession, I noticed my mind didn't appreciate challenges posed to its historical narrative. My mind is innately cynical; therefore, my strong ideological bent was the root challenge. Ideological leaning acts as a kind of shield or first line of defense against new information. That discovery was important, but it didn't fix the problem.

Even if I managed to force my mind to consider alternatives, the deep-seated nature of my mind never truly seemed to change. Newer ideas about meta subjects seemed to always remain in a category of unproven or unprovable, somewhat less in stature than a proven fact. My historical view, a narrative that all reality can be explained eventually, appeared somehow superior. I had managed to move my view of God from a physical to a spiritual reality, but my mind would repeatedly label these ideas as less than a manifest truth.

In summation, my earlier indoctrinated view, a Christian Protestant version of God, had been in the category of a manifest physical truth despite the fact that I was too ignorant to explain the specifics. My new and current idea of God, a spiritual truth centered on Trinitarian philosophy, will never be an irrefutable fact, regardless of any person's wisdom. Though I didn't immediately recognize what had occurred, I had segregated my reality into two realms with this revelation and adopted a kind of dualistic view. My ideology changed in a very fundamental manner.

As I continued to reflect, I noted my internal conflict—if not cognitive dissonance—when I dared attempt to admit a new idea. I was generally a person who would ridicule what I perceived as bizarre. Regardless, I was obsessed with meta subject matter and spent endless hours researching any number of related subjects. This made no sense. I found it upsetting that my tendency was to disrespect such ideas even as I eagerly read the latest release by any number of authors I followed. As time passed, these newer meta ideas seemed somehow better than the old ones. Though they weren't quite internalized the same way as my historical truths the knowledge gave me comfort. I seemed to be enlightened but still lying to myself. I repeatedly failed to integrate the new information into my mind-myth and tacitly remained loyal to my historical narrative. Through ultra-thinking, I would soon figure out why.

In short, I had "daddy issues," just like my older sister had once told me. Siblings provide valuable feedback. I needed to stop attempting to make peace between my sisters and fix my own drama.

I was raised in a religious household that had very distinct views of God and the history of all his people. Those views were simply a reflection of my society, a region of the southern United States called the Bible Belt. Growing up I was specifically told that God was literally true, and this was a fact. Being very left-brain oriented as I matured, I came to believe in a unified theory of truth; one absolute and very physical reality. The methodology of science made sense to me and I naturally assumed all truth could be viewed as an objective set of facts. If you ponder the dynamic you may notice the inherent contradiction; the meta idea of God is forced to exist within a physical reality. Had I not been so left-brain-oriented and obsessive, I probably could have ignored this contradiction for a lifetime; however, that's not how things worked out.

My brain informed me that the methodology of science was a worthy process. This implied that if God could not be objectively proven, then there was, in fact, no God. However, the very early roots of my mind-myth were locked, indoctrinated in a belief that God does exist, and he has a very specific and material nature. My mind only remained peaceful by ignoring this contradiction. When I decided to study ancient cultures with the enthusiasm only a very obsessive person would have, I inadvertently forced my mind to resolve this fundamental contradiction in logic.

Though I didn't notice at the time, this internal struggle came to a head at the passing of my father. My parents, then and now, command a preeminent position within my mind. They along with my grandmother set the boundaries for my own internal story, or mind-myth. Those boundaries were a reflection of the society of my childhood. Even in my thirties, Dad continually reminded me of our boundaries. Having been blessed with the only true version of truth, we dared not question. Again, I stress this message was a message given with love from a community who sincerely had my personal best interest at heart. With the utmost respect for my father, my inclination was to accept his version of the truth as he had done from the same community decades before. This seemed to have given me the courage to ignore a rather obvious flaw in my own logical mind. When he passed, my mind was left alone in defense of this historical narrative.

Always revisiting my obsession with ancient cultures, I kept urging my narrative toward an acceptance of more rational views. I couldn't seem to truly become enlightened and decided it was Dad's fault. Failing to appreciate that he too had been a victim of indoctrination promoted by that same society, I resented him personally as well as myself. Through my own twisted logic, the courage he provided was somehow to blame for my ignorance.

I can admit today that throughout most of my God-journey, deep down I considered myself a spiritually vacant agnostic, simply too afraid to call myself an atheist and be done with the whole issue. I was never particularly happy on my quest, still much of the time I found the drama rather funny. After all, I had plenty of wonderful friends who didn't seem to ponder God in the least. On further reflection, I didn't so much resent my upbringing as admire how well my family and society had programed my mind. I seemed to be a rather well-adjusted productive member of Western society, yet I still had a problem; my obsessive nature. The reflection continued.

Thinking through the issue I decided that somehow, I had simply elected the truth of my father although logically his view was far less plausible than most of the alternatives. Within my personal narrative I was expressing respect for my father to such an overwhelming extent that my tendency is to deny the most likely conclusion (the existence of God can't be proven) in favor of my father's conclusion (the existence of God <u>has</u> been proven). For me to keep my father on a pedestal, my biased mind-myth seeks to deny any belief that calls Dad a fraud. That subconscious choice caused tremendous stress and angst in my life for decades. The Ultrathoughts then followed: The mind is truly dominant of all that I consider a truth, and there is no absolute truth.

Most of us who seek to understand our own Godhead design have a story, and that's mine. Obviously, my quest was more of a fistfight than a wonderous journey toward enlightenment. My father versus Hancock, Schoch, and West. His delusion versus theirs, with me the referee. I ruled in favor of my dad, and to you, I admit I fixed the fight. Now that the shouting is over and the protests have been filed I can move on down the trail. I respect my father's right to believe as he did but his view of God is no longer my own.

Admission of my bias nature opened the floodgates, freeing my mind in the process. I can make capricious decisions and when needed I can even say; "It is, because I think it is." In my ultra-thinking of the Godhead I shall be allowed to have faith with no proof because it is very likely that the Godhead is primarily, and possibly entirely meta. I have finally created my Ultrathoughts on God.

If you want more specifics on those ideas as well as some other weird notions about science, I hope you join me in the next book, *Forbidden Philosophy*.

CHAPTER 2

WHY BOTHER TO THINK?

This series advances the theory that thought is good for our species. Furthermore, I assume that we on this planet this day are the only creature capable of deep contemplation. Obviously, I have no proof of my belief nevertheless I elect this truth. I didn't simply make this up, I actually did years of casual research and ultra-thinking on the subjects of evolution and anthropology. One very important thing that I discovered was that it's sometimes hard to distinguish the bones of our species from those of another version of hominins (human-like great apes). In fact, anthropologists have often been forced to rewrite reference material to reflect new information. What was once thought to be *Homo heidelbergensis* or *Homo neanderthalensis* (a.k.a. Neanderthal) quietly becomes reclassified as *Homo sapiens* or vice versa. As scientists have refined the use of DNA sequencing in its application to ancient bones the problem occurs less often, but it does still occasionally happen. Anthropologists still have a difficult time distinguishing the bones of our species from other animals.

There is far more that makes a species than bones. We use sophisticated tools and advanced speech, we walk taller, our hands have more dexterity, and it is believed our mental capabilities far exceed other animals including all other hominins. Of course, we've never tried to talk with a Neanderthal or any other hominins, but if we did, anthropologists tell us we would be attempting to speak with little more than a fool. It is supposed we are far superior. Count me as skeptical with regard to that belief, but I'll give the experts their due. In fact, I will call their truth mine for now.

A review of our advantages over other animals (i.e., tool use, speech, walking, thinking) highlights a problem on the horizon. Won't machines be able to overtake our supposed advantages fairly soon? From casual observation it seems obvious to me that basically all of those advantages will soon be ceded to robots or artificial intelligence. So . . . what then? What will continue to make us special?

Our capacity for deep contemplative thought is what many believe is our true distinction as a species. I suggest there is no topic more appropriate for such effort than contemplation of the Godhead. In order to successfully contemplate a subject like God, one must first seek freedom from preexisting ideology. If the subject is not approached in this manner you will likely find yourself simply reinforcing your current perspective. In such a case, what's the point? For this reason, deep consideration of meta subjects, philosophy, and the Godhead are ideally suited for ultra-thinking.

Recognition that you have an ideology is the first step toward successful ultra-thinking. Each of us has a bias, an ideology. It develops naturally over time though it can be guided with intent. Your current outlook started with your orientation to think more rationally or more imaginatively. As you mature, this often-subtle influence present within your DNA comes to seriously skew your personal narrative. This leaning mind-myth presents itself as the way you think. Your truth and your very reality are made manifest in your presentation to the world. In a sense we are each a victim of our innate brain leaning. That being the case, it is at least possible that our version of truth is insufficient. Purposeful ultra-thinking is beneficial in its attempt to free the mind so it may think from the whole brain, not one given hemisphere. Biasness is restrained while ultra-thinking.

Ultra-thinking is far more difficult than it may first sound. Those fully immersed in their ideology often don't have the slightest awareness of its influence on the quality of their thoughts or ideas. In book one of the series, *Intentional Thought*, I pressed the point repeatedly that reality is self-created and reinforced by the ideology of the mind. To foster an open mind, one must consistently maintain awareness that reality is simply a mental construct. Fail to appreciate this very reasonable supposition and you just may lose the ability to think beyond your predisposition.

Our reflexive view, an inherently biased view of our truth, is our personal reality. While this is neither good nor bad on the surface, we should appreciate that our impressions or sets of truths are not necessarily fair-minded opinions. You and I each live "a" reality, but not "the" reality. I am not presenting a concept that purports that there is no physical reality and we're all living in a matrix or simulation. The point made is that our individual narrative controls our interpretation of reality. A physically based or objective truth may exist, but if said fact is not internalized within the mind as a truth, the point is rendered moot. In effect, all is an illusional truth of mind, a delusional reality.

Unlike classical whole-brain thinking, which typically seeks to build on what you've already learned, the ultra-thinking method seeks to build from scratch. The thinker in our premise is attempting to engage a brain devoid of baggage, preconceptions, partialities, and even existing formal knowledge. The assumption being, forethoughts are innately biased thoughts and will lead to skewed conclusions.

In book one of the series, we learned of a biological source of ideological leaning: the innate function of our brain. Every individual brain leans to be oriented toward either logic and structure or creativity and flexibility. The extent of the leaning varies to one degree or another; nevertheless, your brain is oriented toward the logical-left hemisphere or creative-right hemisphere. Given these predispositions, over time many of us will mature to become extremely dogmatic in our view of the world. As a result, we can't help but disrespect the opinions of others. They are wrong, and we are right pursuant to our unique delusion.

A logical-left leaning Old General or creative-right leaning Old Hippie is what I call an ideologically immersed individual. These characters would find it difficult if not impossible to ultra-think. Assuming our two characters are left to their own disposition and solely interact with like-minded individuals, all's well. Their world view, their truth and reality, is not significantly offended. On the other hand, should these individuals be forced to interact, the end result is obvious.

Without intention to think of a fair and objective mind, there is little doubt that most of us will be victims of leaning. We naturally have a tendency to devalue the views of those who think differently. This is not automatically a problem. Group cohesion is important to societies and this means people, at least to a certain extent, should support their own historical truth and that of their peers. However, enthusiasm for one set of beliefs at the cost of all others can become a major issue. Aggressive denial of all dissent, stifles societal growth, leads to oppression, and hinders the evolution of thought. This is exactly what happened during the period commonly called the "Dark Ages" of Europe. Aristocratic governments partnered with church to deny any alternative points of view and this repressed societal evolution for hundreds of years. In my view it won't be government who brings about our next period of stagnation, it will be us.

Today it has become patently obvious that people are becoming more polarized and driven more by ideology than either brotherly love or reason. This is because we have the ability through technology to isolate ourselves within a reinforcing sphere of beliefs. We don't need to make any real effort to garner support for our own belief. A simple web search will connect you with hundreds of like-minded thinkers. As more of us exclusively surround ourselves within our own biased world view very few fair-minded thinkers will remain.

Your author is an admitted member of Club Left. My orientation is toward a delusional reality, assuming a cosmos filled with reasonable truths. Though I appreciate that my delusion is biased and I can never fully escape, I can work to suppress my ideology enough to consider alternative points of view plausible. By refusing to remain in my own bubble I am electing not to be bound by my innate predisposition. It's certainly not always comforting to force myself to seriously consider what, at first blush, appears to be foolish opinions. However, I'm not a serious person by nature and if I can keep the discussion light-hearted I can pretty much tolerate anybody who's not aggressive in defending their own view. Aggression, frankly most any emotion, indicates the person has switched into 'ideology mode'. At that point, any further discussion becomes more like a sermon than a 'TED Talk'.

Learning to ultra-think has been tremendously beneficial. If you come to appreciate and practice the approach, it will be of tremendous benefit to you as well. I constantly seek to rethink my truth, particularly as it relates to the Godhead and certain aspects of science. Though I fail more than I succeed, occasionally I come upon what I consider very worthy and well-balanced ideas: Ultrathoughts. As a result, my spiritual health has never been better, and I've come to certain conclusions that seem to be rather enlightened. I am less likely to feel anger when confronted or challenged.

My reality, indeed my very words, may seem rather bizarre to one immersed in their own ideology. I have trained my mind to ultra-think over years. We don't ultra-think using the whole brain by simply becoming aware of bias. In fact, my very use of the terms "bias" and "delusion" undoubtedly creates a touch of anger in some readers. People don't like to be challenged, and certainly don't want to accept an implication that they are somehow deluded. At this point, all I wish to remind you is that I speak out of compassion to you and suggest that if you stick with me through this very short book you just might start to think a bit differently.

To be successful in the process, your mind must allow you to believe that it is plausible, if not probable, that your very reality is a delusion of mind-myth construction. Once this has been accomplished you will find you can somewhat suppress your ideology. Though you will remain under constant attack by your brain's orientation if you continually question your gut response, you will eventually notice your bias. Once you notice your leaning, you will then note that your ideology shades your thoughts.

Through decades of struggle, I discovered what for me has been a number of life-altering Ultrathoughts. I've grown to view all that I know, my reality, as coexisting in two distinct realms. This has been immensely helpful as the approach has allowed me to retain both a logical-left and creative-right view of reality in my mind. In my belief, there are indeed two distinct realms of reality. Each can be valid and has its own set of truths. In book one I used the metaphor of a carnival balloon as a visual representation of these two realms of truth.

Your truth, indeed your reality is unique to you, and you may not prefer to view reality as two realms of truth. If you choose to consider a dimensional multiverse or a purely objective reality, that detail is unimportant. My objective is to urge you to contemplate your truth by presenting my own version alongside the truths of a few others. Certainly, as you will soon read, philosophers have believed in any number of Godhead or reality interpretations. Designs of the Godhead have come and gone. The society of dynastic Egyptians had their theory, and various Greek thinkers had theirs. The philosopher Pythagoras heard music in the cosmos that he associated with the Godhead, while the Egyptians believed their human leaders would become gods.

Occasionally a spiritual religion will evolve from a more generalized Godhead philosophy. As ceremony and tradition intertwine with the basic philosophy, sometimes the original idea is almost overwhelmed by its religion. Not unlike a well written novel, rich details of a religion fix in the mind. For this reason, as time passes people tend to assign more weight to religion than its parent philosophy.

To ultra-think my own truth of the Godhead, I needed to work hard to suppress my leaning. My indoctrination into a particular religion weighed very heavy on my personal narrative. During my quest I researched the Godhead philosophies of others. This took me more than two decades. The creation of Ultra-thoughts is driven by ultra-thinking, but one must still research the subject matter. I read dozens if not more than a hundred books on the subject. My interpretations are summarized here in this volume.

One who is currently not so ideologically immersed in a spiritual religion may find it fairly easy to ultra-think the Godhead. In an odd twist, if you have little spiritual awareness your narrative may be largely free of biasness for or against God. You won't need to first unlearn in order to prepare for enlightenment. Frankly, my journey would have been far less painful had I been so lucky.

Of course, a person who has never contemplated God may be a person extremely biased in favor of the physical realm (objective or knowable reality) and the non-spiritual religion of science. Suppressing an ideology that has elevated the worthiness of science can be every bit as difficult as suppressing an ideology of spiritual religion. Regardless of whether you are immersed in a dense ideology or not, as you read keep in mind that with effort you might ultra-think your way to spiritual enlightenment.

In short, you should care to ultra-think for your own sake. It will help you create a more balanced version of your personal truth. As this happens, you will become a purposeful creation rather than a victim of your reflexive ideological bent.

With that said, I further suggest we owe it to our species to attempt to ultra-think. We are special on the planet today, and yet I look around and see a bunch of materialist auto-humans. They eat, socialize (but only among believers), work, play, and consume. How many philosophers do you know? I've yet to meet one. Without exercising our unique capability, we are in a sense putting ourselves in a cage. Who would deny a jaguar the ability to run, climb, and hunt, to do what it was born to do? Uncage yourself from the zoo that is our society if for no other reason than the simple fun of exercising your mind. That's what we do.

CHAPTER 3

DEFINING GOD

N ow that you have an understanding of the importance of ultra-thinking, and since your courage to think the outrageous has been bolstered, let's push ahead to evaluate some Ultrathoughts of pure philosophy. Philosophy is a contemplation of the nature of knowledge, reality, and existence. The subject is purely meta or nonphysical in nature, and because of this, there are absolutely no incorrect solutions to problems pondered. The topic is ideal for ultra-thinking.

With a liberated whole-brain thinking mind, let's consider the nature of truth with regard to the Godhead as contemplated in the Mediterranean region for several thousand years. This is truly the ultimate big topic that intimidates many, but not you. I will be covering a tremendous amount of material in very few words, so feel free to stop and research it (Google it) if I have confused you. If you wish to read a vigorous academic thesis on the history of philosophy, this is not the book for you. The point of this book is to familiarize you with the subject matter and show you that opinions vary. This work will educate your narrative and hopefully urge your current delusion toward further inquiry. Theoretically if you challenge your existing views the quality of your delusion should improve.

When considering the philosophical concepts of individuals who lived hundreds or even thousands of years ago, we must take time to always consider the culture of the historical author. Without understanding how the texture of society influences each word written, you risk misinterpreting the philosophy. Words carry the societal baggage of both the author and the reader, which subconsciously influence interpretations. Just as we experience a breakdown in communication when attempting to translate a foreign language without a cultural understanding, we often miss an author's point without some basic understanding of the historical era in which they lived. We should likewise be aware of their writing style if we seek to read a literal translation of an ancient work. One may understand the words, but the style of writing could make the message almost incomprehensible at first read. Only after becoming familiar with the form can the reader begin to catch the tone of the author, and then, after appreciating the society and culture of the era, one can grasp the message.

Given the nature of our topic, it is particularly important that we share an understanding of the definitions of some important words. The terms "Godhead" and "God" are defined in this book as a superhuman presence, force, or spirit that may or may not involve physical matter. The key point is that our definition includes both material and spiritual natures. Although today we tend to automatically consider concepts of God to be a metaphysical topic, many if not most of the early philosophers never thought it necessary to make a distinction between the spiritual and physical. Such segregation of the concept would only become common hundreds if not a thousand years after Plato developed his most lucid Ultrathoughts. Eons ago, people's daily experiences weren't segregated into realms; so, when considering ancient beliefs, we must appreciate that their concept of God was probably quite different than our own. Therefore, as we think about their worship of a specific idol, statue, or temple associated with a god we should be mindful not to fall into our preconceived notions.

We are tempted to believe that the Greeks or Romans revered some specific statue as if it literally was the actual god. Even the word *literal* is a bit of a misnomer. *Literal* implies the existence of the physical. If one doesn't ponder a difference between meta and physical, there is no point to the word *literal*. When we ultra-think the culture and mindset of the populous of the time, we probably should appreciate that the physical statue was merely a further representation of the concept. This distinction is important if we are to gain a more complete understanding of the philosophy during this era. Make no mistake—to defame the statue was to defame the god in the mind of the believer. Nevertheless, the physical rock of the statue was not the god.

Religious practice often involves a very specific physical item or place. Just as a statue or specific temple may be extremely important conceptually, a place may represent the same. The concept of God is timeless, but the physical representation of a god often becomes a focal point for religion. Rituals, ceremonies, and traditions blend with philosophy. An overarching dogma of religious belief is the result. Eventually, within the mind of the believer, little distinction is made between the physical representation of a god and the god in concept. Statue, idol, temple, or spiritual presence of God were conceptually all "the God," and no distinction is made regarding the physical or spiritual nature of the deity.

Let's now consider the word *soul*, whether human or animal. In most philosophies, an individual soul must at some point be partnered with a living organism. That partnership lasts for the life of the living, at which point the soul typically does one of two things: reincarnate to then partner with a different living organism or seek the Godhead. Seeking the Godhead can result in success (sometimes called heaven) or failure (sometimes called hell). Soul always has a nonphysical or spiritual component. A common method to describe the soul today is to make a distinction between the physical body (the individual) and the nonphysical presence of the body (the person). Conceptually similar to mind-body dualism, this view is not universally accepted.

Further developing this dualistic view, some Godhead philosophies even identify the physical location of the spiritual soul. Some of the more common ideas of the soul's location are the pineal gland deep in the brain, the brain in general, or the heart. More popular today is the idea that the soul has no specific location when partnered; it is merely a vaporous spirit force, and that spirit is either inside or around the living organism. The point is that it is a mistake when contemplating ideas of the soul to automatically assume the soul as only a spiritual entity that exists for the benefit of man. Conceptually, souls can be for people, animals, the cosmos, or any combination. At least one-third of the population of our planet (and about half of the philosophers discussed in this book) consider that both people and animals have some type of soul or life force presence.

Our third consideration is the term "world soul." This spiritual concept is very common in some parts of the globe, but not so much in Western society. There are numerous descriptions of the term, but for our purpose world soul is best considered a universal energy or life force. In most ancient philosophies it exists apart from the perfect Godhead as a distinct presence that may or not fully mirror its source. In more modern interpretation it includes concepts like "Mother Earth" and or the background energy of the cosmos. So-called "new-age circles" often integrate the concept within their Godhead designs. The idea of a collective mind is often associated with the world soul idea.

As a general rule, believers in a world soul don't consider my view of reality to be their truth. Believers often refer to a type of multi-dimensional reality rather than a dual reality comprised of both a physical and spiritual realm. World soul believers tend to consider all reality as one thing. Their reality has blended the physical and meta together. There is then no delineation. God-head, man, matter, energy, and the universe are all one reality.

The following summaries presented here will continue to encourage you to ultra-think about all subjects, not simply the Godhead. Meta subjects in general are among my personal favorites for a very special reason. Thoughts of the meta will never be proven wrong. Plato—yes, Plato himself—can't be proven right any more than you can. His ideas are not superior to yours. Only you validate your truth and there will never be absolute definitive proof of God. Most of the philosophers discussed here seemed to appreciate the irony that their own attempts to explain everything explained nothing but their own mind.

I do my best not to editorialize too much on their ideas. But then again, I am a product of my leftward leaning. If you're interested in my personal philosophy I hope you pick up the third and final book in the series, *Forbidden Philosophy*.

CHAPTER 4

AN EGYPTIAN FOUNDATION

Now that some groundwork has been laid in defining *God*, *soul*, and *world soul*, let's consider one of the earliest and best-documented descriptions of the Godhead and its relationship to the human soul: the Egyptian funerary texts colloquially called the *Book of the Dead*. Possibly dating as far back as 2600 BCE and evolving over several hundred years, the Egyptians vividly represented their version of the afterlife and in doing so described how an individual relates to the Godhead after death. Of course, the Egyptians can't be credited with having invented the concept of God, but their Ultrathoughts, pounded into rock many millennia ago, helped provide the foundation for an untold number of thinkers to come. Dynastic Egyptians documented Ultrathoughts that presented the journey of a soul from birth through the afterlife. This soul was not exclusive to humans, but it was only a human who played an active role in guiding his or her soul.

Egyptologists instruct us how to interpret their philosophy and associated religion. Accordingly, if the soul's physical partner had led a proper and moral life, the soul could at the death of its partner elevate to reside in the Field of Reeds (or Offerings) with the rejuvenated body of the dead. This is the goal of every soul— to reside in the land of plenty for eternity. The afterlife, being a physical place occupied by both the soul and body, would require that individuals have access to their dead physical body, which is why the Egyptians didn't cremate their dead; they preserved them, kept their vital organs in jars, and provided everyday items for future use by the deceased.

This planning for the afterlife journey and post-death experience was particularly important at the death of a Pharaoh, which is why we find so many treasures, and even an occasional slave, buried with each of them. The passing of a Pharaoh, an earthly demigod (minor god, or person with god-like presence), was thought to influence the entire world for eternity, so the successful navigation through the afterlife by any Pharaoh was of interest to every Egyptian. The death of a wicked Pharaoh, or even a Pharaoh not well prepared for the afterlife, could result in natural disasters or even a failure of the sun to rise. In such a case, the living Egyptian would know that an evil demon prevailed in the underworld because the dead Pharaoh had failed Egyptian society by not being worthy in his or her afterlife.

Every Egyptian, Pharaoh or not, was evaluated at death by the gods of the cosmos. Credible sources instruct us that the heart of the departed would be weighed on a scale against a feather. Egyptologists tell us we are to assume the ancient Egyptians were speaking of the actual human heart given the fact that hearts and other organs have been mummified.

The heart represents the location of the eternal soul. Should this soul be too heavy and tip the scale from the feather, the soul would then sink to its proper dimension in the underworld with each level being successively worse than the former. This hell, for lack of a better term, was dominated by the demon Ammit, the "Swallower of the Damned." A light heart would avoid hell. A light heart was a clean heart, and it would rise when weighed against the feather to enjoy eternal bliss. A Pharaoh must have a light and pure heart free of the weight of evil to be a success in the afterlife for the sake of his people.

Authorized Egyptologists (the Egyptian government must authorize one to speak of history) maintain that their ancient society believed literally in the teaching of the *Book of the Dead*, although many unofficial sources disagree. Authorized presenters point out that the mummification process and storage of goods necessary for a physical existence in the afterlife clearly indicate the Egyptians took their interpretation literally. They urge us to ask, what is the point of preserving a body if the body isn't used in the afterlife?

The afterlife journey as described dates to at least 2400 BCE and includes boats, oxen, servants, etc. All these items have been found buried with Egyptians, which certainly lends credence to the idea that they took this story quite literally. However, we can never be fully confident in our interpretations of what they truly believed. Like the painted murals presenting scenes from the *Book of the Dead*, when we view their representations of the bird-headed god, Horus, are we to automatically assume they literally believed in such a creature? I'm not so sure.

Societies of people four or five thousand years ago certainly promoted various truths that we may characterize as colorful fantasy, but these people weren't gullible fools. So, when you ultra-think about ancient designs of the Godhead and the afterlife, keep in mind we're all the same species, starting with an appreciation that the ancients were intelligent. They were rational thinkers who used logic to deduce cause and effect relationships. Absent quality data and proven formulas, they made assumptions. We don't know what they did or how they understood their world, but a quick look at their massive structures certainly informs us that they knew the difference between physical matter and meta ideas. They couldn't have built much of anything on the Giza plateau, not having understood the difference between fact and fiction.

Key to your acceptance of my supposition is to be aware that ancient minds didn't see a need to distinguish the physical from the spiritual as we do today. Physical and meta exist. They always have; they always will; but they were jumbled together rather seamlessly within the mind of a person two, three, or even a hundred thousand years ago. When allegory was used neither the author or audience dwelt on whether the story was meant to represent a clear statement of physical fact or a fantastical story. Think of it this way: There was no fiction section in the libraries of ancient Egypt. The author merely wanted to convey a message, nothing more, and the audience simply didn't think as we do with regards to the Godhead.

Certainly, I'm in the minority, but I simply look at the larger point of the Egyptian afterlife story: The eternal future of the soul is affected by the action of the living person. In my view, this *is* the story. Remember, that any philosophy is by definition not a literal set of truths. And, religion, even that of the ancient Egyptians is fundamentally an expression of Godhead design. I, therefore conclude that in sacred writings the journey of the eternal soul is being represented in allegory, and any physical accompaniments of burial are simply pomp and circumstance of an associated religion. The food, the organs, the oxen, all of these accompaniments are a kind of diorama constructed in commemoration of the holy story. Egyptian funerary texts, call them the *Book of the Dead* if you prefer, tell the tale of a metaphysical journey through the spiritual realm.

We must be careful in our descriptions. We reflexively think in black and white terminology. We contrast fact and fiction; truth and allegorical representation. Ancient peoples didn't bother to make such clear distinctions. To believe as the society believed was far more important than the texture of one's belief. My Ultrathoughts lead me to believe that even the most common of ancient Egyptians, assuming we could convey the question, knew the details weren't literally true. In this case, the only literalists may be the "authorized" Egyptologists and dogmatists of today.

Regardless of whether one accepts my allegorical assumptions or the Egyptologists' literal assumptions, there is no denying that some of the oldest Ultrathoughts of God and soul are documented best in Egypt. It is very possible that certain fundamentals of the Egyptian Godhead design served as the basis for hundreds if not thousands of designs to follow through history.

Moving forward hundreds of years, let's consider the rise of Hellenistic and somewhat earlier Greek philosophy starting in roughly 600 BCE through about 30 BCE. Keep in mind this era begins at least 1,500 years after the first rock carvings of the *Book of the Dead* were created. As with our information on Egyptian beliefs, we have absolutely no precise information, meaning any so-called expert guidance is largely speculative.

Although we're not sure how or exactly why early Greek philosophers were taught Egyptian concepts of the afterlife, certainly they adapted key concepts from the *Book of the Dead* while shunning its very literal ceremonies. This tells me they were taught that the Egyptians' very vivid depictions of a soul's location, processing, and journey were nothing more than representations. This leaves me to wonder why so many insist the ancients believed in literal gods and demonic forces.

It appears that philosophically the Greeks were a bit more sophisticated in their designs than the Egyptians. My ultra-thinking leads me to conclude the Greeks and certainly later Hellenists definitely thought of their gods principally as nonmaterial entities. With that said, like the Egyptians they held beliefs that we would find rather ludicrous today. However, I must pause. Aren't all Godhead beliefs "ludicrous" when pondered within the context of a material world? Don't many of us openly profess a belief that a physical man literally walked on water? But I digress.

With deference to any Godhead belief, I remind myself that as an intelligent person matures, they learn to distinguish certain facts from fantasy. A person raised in the wilderness by wolves matures to understand that rocks don't speak, and physical organs of the body don't magically reunite with a corpse. Yet, that same person might mature to believe in a superhuman presence of an inexplicable nature. I ultra-think that people instinctively understood that Godhead-associated beliefs were somehow different than those associated with material matter subject to cause and effect relationships. It seems a gnawing need for the Godhead exists beyond or despite of our prudent intuition regarding material reality.

A principal point of this account is to stress that reality to the ancients was a seamless blend of spiritual and physical. Concepts we would call meta permeated all truth of old. When these societies created statues of gods, they did so out of respect for their deities. They may have been indoctrinated to believe many "truths" that we would find strange, but I suggest places, temples, and statues weren't literally considered gods in and of themselves. Physical representations of the Godhead became symbols that united the public in a common myth. People united around a belief felt a sense of connection to one another.

Unlike most modern people today, the ancients weren't indoctrinated into a world dominated by science; as a result, it was beyond their frame of reference to ponder whether a ceremony— like sanctifying a statue—actually meant the statue was, in fact, the God. They simply didn't think as we do today. Even the terms *material reality* and *metaphysical reality* had no meaning in their view.

Once the use of the scientific method had spread and the population came to understand that having objective evidence in support of a truth was better than not, the individual mind of the being began to change. Humans then sought more objective evidence and chose to seriously deliberate what could be considered objectively proven or not. The nature and quality of reality itself became an important question.

A reasonable manner to resolve these types of questions is to simply seek more information and knowledge. Once more information is known, the individual can make a better judgment of what was objectively true or real. Knowledge for its own sake then becomes a subject of our desire. He or she obtains a kind of benefit from actually "knowing" a truth. After all, who today doesn't wish to understand more than another? We seem to crave information. Success in obtaining and understanding information becomes a reward for self and a price for ego. This desire pushes people to seek more and more objective facts or irrefutable conclusions.

It is also possible that up until the rise of the Hellenistic culture, the ego itself was inconsequential. Don't misunderstand—I am not saying ego didn't exist. What I am reminding you of is that eons ago very few members of society ever left the social class to which they were born. Without social mobility, the ego would only inflate so far. A person could be egotistical and prideful within their small group, but very few members of a lower class of peasants stood any realistic chance of leaving their social class of birth. As knowledge itself became widely disseminated, the perspective of society probably changed. People could aspire to be more than their simple class of birth. Knowledge itself may have provided an opportunity for the individual. This alone could impact one's self-image. The ego would be inflated. An individual could set themselves apart from the group just by having better or more knowledge. Once knowledge came to be disseminated a sort of competition would arise. When ordinary people could learn and internalize a truth being supported through some sort of objective measure, their self-esteem was amplified, and knowledge itself would become an object of desire.

Supporting this Ultrathought is the fact that those held in highest esteem were the magi, shaman, or holders of knowledge. Their status was obtained because these individuals had knowledge not widely disseminated. This knowledge remained special or even powerful as long as most remained uninformed. A shaman whose information is well understood by others is no longer a revered shaman, but a simple resource for knowledge. Like watching magic. Seeing or "believing" once or twice is fine. But once you have internalized an understanding of the game, the trick is no longer worth watching.

With the rise and further spread of knowledge, societal beliefs became far more diverse and fluid. If a society sought to maintain a meta belief, and that belief came to be ridiculed by knowledge deemed credible, then the society was obliged to segregate spiritual belief from provable truth.

In book one I used the term *MOS* as an abbreviation of the mind of society, or the tone, the attitude of the collective. The MOS, to a large degree, is mentally evaluated by individuals to measure the worthiness of their own existing belief. Since the MOS represents the dominant or default understanding of the group, people are wary about believing something not commonly believed by peers. People prefer to accept the wisdom of the group unless that supposed "wisdom" is simply too offensive to the person. As knowledge comes to be accepted and internalized by the person, such offense is more likely to occur. The significance of the MOS on the individual mind is enhanced as society grows in size, and societal opinion comes to dominate all opinion. Concerning concepts of Godhead, God, or soul, how would an individual or society ever support these meta beliefs when objective evidence becomes the standard in determining all truth?

The Greeks had an answer. They began to segregate concepts within the mind: the likely provable and the likely not provable.

We know this because, without a doubt, people circa 500 BCE were presented with stories of the Godhead and concepts of philosophy that couldn't possibly be believed as literal truth, and yet these people still respected these ideas as a type of truth.

In the case of the Egyptians we can't be certain that they categorically rejected any and all literal interpretation of their Godhead concepts. We are reminded of the mummies of Egypt complete with stores of food and other supplies. While I believe few if any intelligent people would believe literally in a post-life field of reeds, it is possible some did. Some Egyptians may have thought their heart or soul would end up on a scale to be weighed, but certainly no thinking Greek thought their soul, a concept difficult in its own right, was actually going to be transported to the light in the sky we call our moon. The sun, moon, and planets were often referred to in Greek and Hellenist philosophy. The moon might have been thought more than a light, or even terra firma by a handful of ancients; however, it's very unlikely that any thinking Greek would have literally believed a soul would occupy the moon.

In what would become a world dominated by the scientific method, it would eventually become necessary for philosophers advocating a superhuman presence of God to admit full segregation of the spiritual realm from the physical reality. That wouldn't officially come about until well after the widespread acceptance of Aristotelian logic culminating in the work of René Descartes, but this process was beginning to percolate through Ultrathoughts of Western philosophers circa 500 BCE. The Godhead need not be anything other than an idea to be a truth.

Eastern philosophers also began evolving their designs to adapt in a world that would soon be immersed in the scientific method. Ultrathoughts of philosophers like Siddhartha Gautama (Buddha, circa 560 BC–483 BCE—the dates vary by source), who advocated a spiritual awakening and physical detachment, clearly showed he had Ultrathoughts that segregate realms during the era. However, such absolute segregation seemed to lose momentum in the East compared to viewpoints in the West. I am not suggesting one was further evolved than the other. Different dynamics affected each region.

As you can tell, this subject matter is challenging, and god concepts vary significantly. The important point is to appreciate that their concepts may have been intended to be considered in a kind of blended or mixed reality. Allegorical representation versus literal fact of belief is a tricky facet to ponder, particularly when we have limited information on which to rely, and much of what we do have is either fragmentary or thousands of years removed from its source. As we continue, be reminded, I may be offering unsophisticated interpretations of very complex Ultrathoughts. Many of these ancient thinkers were surely absolute geniuses who first described and defended the concepts orally. What depth of thought, written or spoken, has been lost to history?

CHAPTER 5

ARGUING THE GODHEAD

In this book we are ultra-thinking. In doing so we are attempting to free ourselves from ideology or previously held belief. This is not necessarily difficult when we consider ancient beliefs of the Godhead. We haven't been indoctrinated into a set of societal beliefs or any associated ancient religion, so we can review as an outsider. We are nonbelievers with respect to religions practiced by those eons ago. All of that changes once we ultra-think our own personal belief, but for now let's continue to ultra-think the Godhead as it was conceived thousands of years ago by others.

When we consider ancient Egyptian or Hellenistic concepts of God, many of us would immediately visualize the Eye of Horus or things like snake-haired harlots. We should acknowledge that our overall impressions of what ancient people thought are tainted by these preconceived notions. We certainly don't know for sure what they were indoctrinated to believe, or what any individual actually thought of the Godhead for sure. However, to consider what others think of their God, one must deeply examine his or her own impression in the process.

In the context of this discussion we should remember *god(s)* is a representation of a philosophy of a Godhead concept. Zeus, the king of Greek gods who lived on Mount Olympus and whose symbols include lightning bolts and an eagle, was as real to them as the God of Abraham is to a Jewish believer or Brahma is to a Hindu. Real in what sense? We will never know. God is "real" to the believer, and each person's belief is unique to their individual mind. Some believe they could walk up and literally touch their

God, others don't. It is probable that many if not most citizens of old instinctively knew their gods to be represented in fantastical form, just as many Muslims, Hindus, and Christians interpret today.

People then were as intelligent as we are today. So, as we consider the stone statues and temples of old, their "gods", I suggest it is foolish to reflexively assume they thought in the same manner as you. I challenge you to consider what they would think of your own personal God today. What would they say if you told them your God arose from a mortal death? God is real to the believer regardless of the details.

In the context of Ultrathoughts the important part of God is the message, not the details. Remember the actual God, in theory, is representative of a philosophy of the Godhead, at least from the position of an outsider or non-believer. But from the viewpoint of the believer the script is reversed. The philosophy is not so much supporting the God as it is a product of the deity.

Many today find it unimportant to dwell on questions regarding physical presence or acts by god(s). They choose to automatically interpret a god as instructed by elders. They then barely contemplate the philosophy. Religion with its texture and promotion tends to overwhelm a philosophy given enough time. I dare say many believers go through their lives without even knowing an underlying philosophy supports their religion. That is fine when it works, but many people seek a deeper understanding of religion and philosophy. They like to contemplate and debate with others. Such discussions lead to a deeper understanding of the subject. Rhetorical discussion (i.e. a narrative put forth in a manner to persuade the audience) challenges the speaker to refine the argument.

As religions and associated dogma age within a society, they become an important part of the culture. The society supports the religion and the religion contributes to the culture. God traditions, texts, and ceremonies were no less important to the ancients than the Christian Bible is to the culture of the United States or the Quran to the culture of Saudi Arabia. Though they are strange to us, they weren't casual fireside tales; these stories had a point. Their colorful fables bound their people in a common myth that contributed to the success of long-standing cultures. Their fables didn't simply appear; they came about through contemplation and discussion. Over time stories in support of philosophy and associated religions helped create a more cohesive society. A group of people united is a formidable presence in the world, a particularly important characteristic in times of global conflict.

As Greek society evolved it came to respect personal freedom. What is a basic way to express freedom? Speak, and speak loudly in public. Free open-air discussion began to emerge in Greek society more or less 2,600 years ago. With that freedom of speech, lucid Ultrathoughts rhetorically presented in open society started to challenge more established views on the Godhead. Religions of old came under scrutiny. The MOS became malleable in time as society came to appreciate not only the arguments but a person's "right" to think independently of the group.

Unlike a religious leader who had simply relied on the defense of tradition in support of belief, independently-minded philosophers became skilled at argument. The dynamic can be compared to that of a highly skilled attorney arguing with a stodgy bureaucrat about an outdated or irrational interpretation of the law. The old ways of thinking of the superhuman force of the Godhead began to lose favor once society adapted to accept public discourse. The spread of this trend would soon consume not only philosophical discussion of the Godhead but religious dogma itself, leaving society void of any commonly held belief in the Godhead.

Historical views came to be replaced by well-thought-out and lucid ideas of God. Positions had to be defended not by dogma but strength of argument. These new beliefs eventually formed the foundation of newer religions, but just as the old doctrine fell, any new one remained under constant threat of revision.

Philosophers of this period had a very distinct advantage over their predecessors. They had the good fortune to live during a period in history when leaders were beginning to respect freedom of thought by the individual. Open air rhetorical discussion helped thinkers refine their ideas of the Godhead.

Democracy, a political system in which members of society contribute to their own governance, might be first traced to the votes cast by the Spartans, circa 700 BCE, yet it is the philosophers of the city-state of Athens who coined the term and solidified the concept of the rule of the people in 508 BCE. Before this era, elite leadership strictly controlled which views were deemed acceptable by the society. Aristocracy, meaning rule of the elite, was the standard form of governance. Until there became a general acceptance of a person's freedom to debate important issues in public, critique of any ideology promoted by authority was strictly prohibited.

Prior to this period, an elite few protected the status quo to their benefit. Deviation from any sanctioned belief was considered a threat and quickly suppressed. As debate liberated the population under the banner of "All people have a right to think for themselves," it gave some tacit legitimacy to even the most outrageous new concepts of the Godhead. A more laissez-faire style of governance gained a foothold in this era. And, though it is true that Socrates, mentor of Plato, was eventually prosecuted for "corrupting the youth" by a seemingly enlightened society, his government was comparatively receptive to fresh ideas. This less authoritarian style of government allowed rhetoric—the defense of an idea through lecture and discussion—to be practiced. Ideas and Ultrathoughts were brought forth, debated, and refined by open discussion provided they didn't quite cross some ever-moving line of decorum. One who could debate skillfully while pushing the limits of thought obtained influence and superior social status.

Of course, this pendulum of free discussion continued to swing to and fro as the years passed. The trend would eventually cease and even reverse by the seventeenth century. Regardless, the important takeaway is that until the Ultrathought of democracy was conceived and accepted ever so slightly, ideas of the Godhead were relatively stable. A person's idea of the Godhead was probably an indoctrinated set of beliefs passed down for hundreds of years by the ruling elites. Once government and societal attitudes loosened, things started to change. Of course, a person could always think as they chose, but those thoughts were likely "forbidden" until personal liberty came to be respected. As hidden or personal thoughts, these ideas failed to benefit from the critique of outsiders.

Admittedly, democratic or self-ruling concepts are not original ideas of the Greek people. Small tribes walking the Serengeti plains, or the wilds of the Amazon several hundred millennia ago argued in the open air. I have no doubt they took an occasional vote as a means of decision making, no different than a group of children deciding which game to play. But as a group of people becomes larger, exceeding several hundred, control becomes a challenge. Allowing rhetorical discussion in public poses a risk to society.

The easiest and quickest manner to control people is through coercion and the limitation of individual freedoms. This has been the norm since societies of people became rather large. However, once a society adopts some sense of morality that emphasizes that every human life is special, then an informed population will eventually rebel against an oppressive authority. Leadership then has a choice: increase the coercion and repression or seek cooperation from the people. The Athenians formed a well-developed set of Ultrathoughts in an attempt to have a cooperative population. Adoption of this model, first by Greek society and eventually the vast Roman Empire, prompted dozens if not thousands of well-thought-out philosophies throughout the Greco-Roman world. Other societies, like that ruled by the Huns, Genghis Khan, or countless other dictators chose a different route. They chose oppression and control over democracy and liberty.

Part II

CHAPTER 6

A FEW PHILOSOPHERS

To be a philosopher, a privilege historically reserved for nobility, is to live a life of discipline, self-reflection, and contemplation. A philosopher seeks the meaning of existence and generates a new thesis concerning the very nature of truth or challenges an accepted view. A philosopher lives for Ultrathoughts. Much of the foundation of modern civilization is built upon the thoughts of a handful of philosophers who began to gain prominence throughout the western Mediterranean basin starting circa 500 BCE. We will consider some of their revelations, and more importantly, you will learn that even Ultrathoughts of the greatest minds in history were subject to challenge, revision, and scorn. A unique aspect of philosophical thought is that rarely can any general idea be proven unequivocally wrong. Such concepts are well-suited for developing Ultrathoughts of your own.

Working in chronological order, we will consider Pythagoras, Plato, Aristotle, and Stoicism. In the later section, we will move to the Judeo-Christian tradition and talk about Philo, Origen, Plotinus, Augustine, Aquinas, and Descartes. I hope this brief historical recap will help you gain the confidence you need for the challenge of developing Ultrathoughts on these weighty topics.

CHAPTER 7

PYTHAGORAS

Pythagoras is believed to have lived from 570 BCE through 495 BCE. Chronologically, he was one of the first great pre-Hellenistic thinkers and is cited by those who followed as a source of wisdom. Likely born on the small island of Samos, off the coast of modern-day Turkey, his frequent travels afforded him the opportunity to be exposed to a variety of opinions, providing him with important perspective and context. This ultimately gave him and his reputed words gravitas. Those words came to influence the Mediterranean region for hundreds of years.

Though he was a person of modest means, Pythagoras somehow found a way to enhance his studies and was tutored by scholars from Egypt and the eastern cities to which he traveled. He gained an understanding of the concepts of arithmetic from the Phoenicians, geometry from the Egyptians, astronomy from the Chaldeans, and principles of religion from the magi of various cultures. These days most of us are familiar with the geometric formula known as the Pythagorean theorem, where the sum of the squares of the legs of a right triangle is equal to the square of the hypotenuse, but his legacy of math and science is much richer. For example, he either popularized or invented the theory that planets are spherical and that they are moving in a manner that could be represented by various mathematical equations. Let this sink in; it was he who may have first Ultrathought that the movement of planets had nothing to do with the Godhead.

The Egyptian influence on Pythagoras is among the best documented; however, we must note that the history of his education comes to us from material that originated hundreds of years after his death. We aren't fully confident that the information is factual. Many scholars today believe Pythagoras is not worthy of his reputation and status. They note that although he is attributed as a source for Socrates and a revolutionary mathematician, we don't have any actual evidence to support the claims. According to secondhand and thirdhand sources, his initial fame came well after his death. This notoriety resulted from his views on the fate of the soul and his peculiar vegetarian diet.

Some researchers are quite confident that for decades if not more than one hundred years after his passing, Pythagoras did not really have much of any reputation. This adds credence to their argument that he is not really all that special. In fact, these same scholars believe many of the ancient Greek thinkers were basically usurpers of far older Egyptian wisdom.

It is a well-accepted fact that ancient Egyptians closely guarded their ancient knowledge to the extent that it was forbidden to write or disseminate any such information outside of the priesthood. It is entirely possible that we have nothing written by Pythagoras because he was respecting the creeds of his teachers, the Egyptians. In this case, he could have been more of an oral conduit for Egyptian wisdom than an entirely original ultra-thinker. Then as time passed and individuals sought to catalog Egyptian knowledge, with or without forethought scribes simply attributed him as a "source" of said knowledge. I ultra-think it seems obvious that to deny credit to Egyptian thinkers would be to elevate the prestige of the Greek people by attributing Ultrathoughts to Pythagoras.

With that said, I believe certain researchers are a bit too anxious to disrespect the man. We'll never know who thought what first, and it is not impossible that Pythagoras was the preeminent ultra-thinker. Regardless of whether he deserved all, any, or none of the credit, monumental concepts were starting to be shared in a manner that could be understood by more and more people. As one of our earliest rhetorical debaters, his library of thought—inclusive of sophisticated mathematics and the well-known theorem of the right triangle—ultimately came to be called the Pythagorean school of thought.

The subject of mathematics formed the basis from which Pythagoras evaluated what he termed "heavenly bodies" of the solar system. Creating formulas and plotting planetary motion, he characterized mathematical solutions for movement using terms of music. Reputedly he stated that the movements of heavenly bodies produced a music that could be represented through mathematics. He went on to describe that this sonnet harmonized the observed group of spheres to reveal the sound of an exquisite "symphony," and human beings alone possessed the ability to hear such beauty through simple awareness of this mathematical miracle. When persons understand the math, they alone will hear the music. He went so far as to profess that humans exist simply to hear that beauty. For hundreds of years, we naturally assumed that he meant this as a metaphor for the beauty of creation, not an actual audible sound. Today we might paraphrase it by saying that people exist to appreciate the wonder of the universe.

According to Pythagoras, mathematics exists hand in hand with music. Considering his descriptions as metaphors, he not only considered mathematics musical, he spiritualized the specific numbers themselves. Regarding numbers, Pythagoras is credited with saying "All is a number" and "God is a number." In philosophy, numerology is the study of the mystical relationship between numbers and the divine, and—whether his own or adapted from yet unknown ancient sources—numerology is fundamental to many of his core concepts. He found harmony and believed mathematical equations existed throughout nature and the universe; numbers were metaphysical to Pythagoras.

It is worth considering the possibility that his ideas about math and music were not meant as purely allegory or metaphor. Within the last couple of decades, scientists have found that the universe emits actual sound. Incomprehensible until very recently, a vivid example of this music, possibly the music to which he refers, are pulsars. Pulsars are rapidly rotating neutron stars that emit radio and sound waves but absolutely no visible light. These objects couldn't have been discovered without their music. Furthermore, a growing body of evidence appears to support the idea that every living organism, if not every molecule, emits a specific field. This field is a unique signature that can be represented by sound alone. Researchers fervently believe some biological organisms can pick up the sound field of another organism and react to this energy without any other physical interaction. Does this then indicate that Pythagoras was literally speaking of music, sonnets, or fields of sound?

Indeed, it was of keen interest to him that many animals communicate via song. To consider the universe as having a fundamental musical basis, represented by us today in terms of numbers or mathematics, may not be as outlandish as it first appears. Could this have been the true nature of his orally described Ultrathoughts? Recall—we have none of his writing and merely know of his rhetorical statements through written form scribed hundreds of years after his death. Was the nuance of his thought that he, literally, meant actual sound, and that we simply lost this central point in our later translation of his Ultrathoughts? It is plausible that Pythagoras may have known something since forgotten. Was that "something" a reworking of far older Ultrathoughts passed to him by his tutors? Did this one man have some sort of ancient wisdom concerning fundamental music or fields of sound related to the cosmos?

Some researchers theorize that the lost technology of prehistory was the sophisticated use of sound and music. They suggest that through manipulation of sound, the builders could soften, lift, and cut stone. Pythagoras was tutored by countless individuals representing extraordinary ancient wisdom. He apparently assimilated various concepts in the formation of his Ultrathoughts. If we could query him today, how would he clarify his concepts? What if this person was taught that the key to understanding the mysteries of the universe, the cosmos, and all reality lay in an appreciation of actual sounds?

Regarding his consideration of math and music, perhaps some of his elucidations were meant literally and others as allegory. We can't be sure which is which, but when considering his design of the Godhead, his philosophy regarding the nature of the soul, one would have to assume his ideas are meant as allegorical representations. For Pythagoras, the cosmos is structured on a moral principle. This is clearly a metaphysical concept. He stated that heavenly bodies are engaged in a battle between good and evil, with the formulas of mathematics harmonizing and allowing cooperation between the participants. Our sun and moon are the preferred destinations for the soul. Alternatively, in Tartarus (Hell) souls are tormented by evil, fear, and thunder. During life, the soul resides (partners) with the body, which strives for a moral existence, but upon physical death, it must embark upon a journey that most often leads to multiple reincarnations (or second chances, we might say). This is where he clearly distinguishes his specific views from those of the ancient Egyptians.

The soul's second chance could result in a partnership with a human or animal. Should success be finally obtained, the soul may experience a righteous end by stopping the reincarnation cycle and rejoining God. Souls in a reincarnated form never remember a previous life. This idea is often thought to have formed the basis from which Plato developed his more thorough concepts, but I must again stress that almost everything directly credited to Pythagoras is subject to debate.

Unlike the Egyptians, who referred to the Field of Reeds and prepared a corpse for the afterlife experience, Pythagoras said that the sun and the moon were the destinations of the soul. While we may debate whether when he spoke of music he meant real sounds or not, it is extremely unlikely that he believed a soul would physically go to an actual place like the moon. Remember, throughout ancient history, it is probable that people in general didn't consider the moon itself to be a physical thing; after all, the moon was something one saw in the sky, no different than some ill-defined light or light of the stars.

In my view Pythagoras, by framing his concept of God and soul in the non-material realm, effectively documents that the Greeks were considering the Godhead as being metaphysical in substance. The Godhead and the spiritual represent a dimension outside of the physical world. For millennia the world had created rich mythology complete with bizarre gods and stories where the physical and spiritual blended, but by circa 500 BCE, a transition toward segregating the realms had begun to appear. This would become ever more important as people came to demand objective proof in support of a concept. Clearly, it became important to use allegory in the representation of the Godhead. Otherwise, rational debate would render all concepts of the Godhead, God, and soul moot.

CHAPTER 8

PLATO

A few decades after Pythagoras, Greek society had come to embrace the idea of free and open rhetorical debate. Leaders listened to these discussions and, provided they themselves or their interests weren't directly offended, thinkers were granted liberty to debate issues. Eventually, many thinkers did go too far. Socrates was forced to commit suicide, and Plato was sold into slavery for a time. Still, promotion of fresh and well-conceived ideas, Ultrathoughts, became a sport of sorts during the era of Plato.

A skillful master of debate and thought creation could become a recognized celebrity. The best could cleverly support even the most outrageous supposition. While Socrates was an artful practitioner, his star pupil Plato (428 BCE–348 BCE) would ultimately provide the foundation of Western philosophy. During his lifetime he created an impressive catalog of eloquent Ultrathoughts. Using Socrates as the protagonist in his writings, Plato interpreted and reinterpreted what we consider core philosophical questions, providing a lucid starting point for our discussion of the very nature of reality. He is first among those who provided a foundation for our consideration of what we define as metaphysical study. Every single philosopher who has pondered reality is evaluated within the context of Plato. In truth, he probably wasn't the first and may not have even been the best philosopher to ever walk the planet. Yet, he has represented the field for nearly 2,500 years and will most likely be our champion for years to come.

Plato may have been the first advocate of ultra-thinking in hopes of producing Ultrathoughts, though he never knew our word for it. His exact quotes are somewhat muted in translation, but we can paraphrase two of his more important conclusions: "Thoughts are good for the person," and, "One must think to truly know oneself." Plato was certain that a quest for mental clarity would serve to repel base animal instincts. One who fails to seek such wisdom would live a frustrated life—a life in search of endless animal pleasures. Knowledge sought and gained breeds confidence and maturity in man. Each is a quality critical to a successful life.

Through ultra-thinking, Plato developed Ultrathoughts like his monumental theory of forms. He believed that forms are things in themselves and can exist apart from the objects they describe.

For instance, the word *apple* can mean a natural fruit or a shape. The shape of an apple can be imagined without visualizing the fruit. Therefore, *apple* is a quality of its own form. It can be the real, physical apple or a potential form of abstract thought. Since the abstract thought of *apple* is grounded in representation based on the physical apple, it is a quality. To say that something has an apple shape is to represent a form without the specific object. *Apple* has a metaphysical presence.

On the other hand, consider something like the word *beautiful* as in "a beautiful sunset." Beauty is a form having an existence. We can ponder beauty, but we could not describe beauty as tied to a specific object. Furthermore, we won't always agree that a sunset is an absolute beauty, unlike our agreement on the shape of an apple. Note the difference, and then contemplate the implication of the distinction.

The theory of forms explores the nature of things and attempts to bring structure to concepts that deal with what is "real."

Real can, therefore, be meta real or physically real. Ultrathoughts of this type document what we consider the earliest detailed descriptions of the nature of reality. Before one can attempt to contemplate the nature of reality, one must create a foundational definition. The theory of forms is that foundation.

Going beyond the nature of reality, Plato moved forward to consider God or the Godhead. His designs are intertwined with his philosophy concerning the soul. Plato interpreted the nature of the soul by what is called the tripartite theory of the soul. As one considers his concept it may help to visualize a pyramid consisting of several segments, loosely divided into three more general levels. The soul occupies a level on the pyramid. The upper segment is closest to God, and to have one's soul positioned at this highest level is the goal of all souls. The soul, whether that of human or animal, is bonded in partnership to a physical body. That body is bound to a level in the tripartite throughout the physical life. Upon the death of the physical body, the soul is briefly freed, only to be rebound to a newly born physical body of God's predetermination. The freed soul links to a body in status equal to its moral worthiness. For instance, the physical body of a snake is positioned lower on the pyramid than the physical body of a person born into nobility. The freed soul proceeds to partner with a body placed on either a higher or lower level than the soul had occupied previously, with the status of the new life-form partnership depending on the actions of the previous life. Live a subpar life (for Plato, a life without the pursuit of knowledge, simply following animal instincts), and the person's soul is condemned to reincarnate into a lower life-form body.

Much like the ancient Egyptians, Plato believed that the body contaminates the soul through experiences on earth. Immerse your body in the contaminants of the physical, and the soul suffers at your death. All souls start out pure, whether partnered with a snake or a king, but over time must filter everything the body encounters, and the filter becomes heavy with impurities. Only a human life can assist the soul through honorable pursuits, quests for knowledge, and by shunning animal instincts. The system resembles the Egyptian scale concept but with a significant difference. The Egyptians had believed that once the heavy, dirty heart was weighed on the scale, this was the end: the Field of Reeds or a level of hell. For the Egyptians, there was no reincarnation. In Plato's system, very much like Pythagoras more than a hundred years before, the soul keeps having chances to improve or fail through rebirths in new bodies.

In his design, Plato theorized that a quality human being could continually improve the lot of his or her soul in the next iteration (rebirth). Reincarnation provides an opportunity to move up the pyramid, getting closer to God. This being the case, human beings must accept responsibility for their soul. This is where he distinguished himself from his predecessor: People make a conscious decision to defy God and endanger the soul by submitting to animal lusts. Or, they can elect to honor God and help the soul through resisting animal impulses in favor of the pursuit of knowledge.

CHAPTER 9

ARISTOTLE

The most famous student of Plato was Aristotle (384 BCE–322 BCE). We credit him as the father of logic. Of course, calling him specifically *the* father might be a bit of a stretch. Certainly, he couldn't have been the first to think logically. It seems rather obvious that humans use logic automatically. But he was likely among the first to write down a detailed methodology offered as a framework applying logic for the purpose of studying. His methodology was eventually disseminated and synthesized into what we call today the scientific method—experimentation in a manner that is repeatable and standardized.

Being exceedingly prolific and having boundless energy, Aristotle created science for innumerable fields of study. Obsessed with what could be known or not through empirical evidence provided by experimentation, Aristotle built on Plato's theory of forms and applied scientific concepts to the physical world of tangible wonders, such as how the blood flows in the body or why the tide rises. Through a systematic process, he took time to describe fire, motion, optics, and astronomy. Regarding biology, he distinguished over five hundred animal species through a method of taxonomy using genus and species similar to that which we still use today. Most of these animals he personally examined and dissected, explaining the functions of their anatomy in the process. In all likelihood he examined fossils and had some idea as to their origin. His methods were incredibly accurate and descriptive. Writing 2,300 years ago, he provided basic scientific facts in a manner still taught in college courses today.

Again, I must pause to stress that it is entirely possible that Aristotle himself may not have composed all of the ideas to which he is given credit. Like Pythagoras, he was quite familiar with far older designs presented by the ancient Egyptians. In his case he was specifically charged with educating the young Greek prince Alexander the Great. Did Aristotle compile information from Egyptian sources to be used for the education of a prince? Did the Greeks seek to deny any credit to Egyptians and attribute undue credit to Aristotle himself? Be reminded that Alexander the Great conquered Egypt, renaming its key port "Alexandria" in the end. Obviously, the Greeks sought to put their mark on history and disparage the defeated in the process.

With the above sidebar acknowledged, Aristotle sought to describe observations. In doing so he created the idea of starting with an educated guess, or hypothesis. Prior to his musings, people made observations and undoubtedly knew or proved any number of basic facts, but it was Aristotle who set forth a set of facts relating to specific observations or processes that could be repeatedly and methodologically proven in a manner that was easily understood. The end result was that producing repeatable experiments and seeing a scientifically based proof became fundamental to the topic of science itself.

Differing from his master Plato on at least one key point, Aristotle used a modified theory of forms when evaluating reality. Using the apple analogy, he would have argued the apple form doesn't exist without the object regardless of the logic of Plato. Aristotle described and, for all practical purposes, created physics. He was most interested in that which he could prove was a physical reality. In describing "being," he stated it exhibits four causes: material (stuff), formal (shape), efficient (the builder or agent), and final (that which you see). To understand the causes is to understand the being. This focus on the physical being led him to determine that metaphysics is something that exists beyond physics, beyond these causes. In fact, he was the first to coin the term metaphysics.

Through the application of logic, he evaluated metaphysics, relegating it to the otherworldly spiritual realm. In his Ultrathoughts, he describes that God is deemed necessary since reasonably there needs to be some sort of prime or "first mover" of everything. Logic told him that God was required even if never proven since movement is the product of action. Something, even if it could not be understood, must have started everything according to Aristotle. But without physical proof offered by the application of the scientific method, the topic would remain meta, as he called it—outside of physics. Aristotle's Ultrathoughts are so important that many view him, not Plato, as the most important philosopher of history.

CHAPTER 10

STOICISM, AN EVOLUTION OF ARISTOTELIAN LOGIC

A discussion of knowledge and truth grounded by Aristotelian logic would be incomplete without addressing the school of thought best described as a logical morality—Stoicism. Today we consider Zeno of Citium (circa 336 BCE), a Hellenistic thinker, to be among the first Stoics. He was reputedly an ascetic of gloomy disposition. Most credit him as the founder of the Stoic school of philosophy in Athens. As a testament to the common sense nature and universal appeal of the philosophy of Stoicism, many who are students of philosophy are struck by its obvious similarities to the philosophy of Confucius, circa 551 BCE. It is also possible Zeno was familiar with the writings or rhetorical discussions of Plato or his pupil, Aristotle. Aristotle was a contemporary of Zeno. When we note that both Confucius and Aristotle represented substantially similar ideas to those credited to Zeno, we're again left with an unanswered question: What one individual truly originates any philosophical Ultrathought?

Today we view a person who seeks to follow stoic principles in their life, a Stoic, as either a naturalist or rather agnostic thinker. Given this modern interpretation people are often surprised to learn that as originally conceived, Stoicism accepted the Godhead. It was not a philosophy that denied the meta. It was not a non-spiritual religion. Original Stoic Ultrathoughts conceived of the Godhead all that is matter in the universe. The rock, the camel, the sea—they're all part of the Godhead in this interpretation, reminding us yet again that the ancients didn't segregate reality into realms. Matter is all that is known or knowable to the classical Stoic. The unknown or meta was not specifically denied as it is in our modern view of reality. So-called "divine reason" was a real thing to Zeno and his followers.

Individuals as material stuff are de facto part of God in the philosophy. However, people are unique among the other stuff of God and the universe. Only they (living persons) can dominate other physical matter. Individual humans, by definition then, lie as a potential force in opposition to God. Fortunately, humans can choose to act morally and resist animal urges, which pleases the universe or God. To act in harmony with the universe should be the goal of every human.

At death, people degenerate or are consumed by divine fire to become one with the broader material stuff of God. People, like all life, are ultimately recycled to the simple carbon of the earth only to have this matter reemerge at an undefined point in time. In Stoic philosophy, neither person nor animal has a soul. To master life, one must restrain all animal pursuits and promote universal harmony to please the universe of God.

Stoic Ultrathoughts gained traction in Greco-Roman society as these very appealing concepts came to be known throughout the Mediterranean basin. The leadership gained prestige amongst the people by adopting this philosophy, which struck the population as the ultimate expression of fairness. A quasi-democratic government built on a moral foundation not only made sense, it inherently kept the powerful in check.

On this foundation, Marcus Aurelius came to personify Stoicism. Marcus Aurelius would be known as one of the last good emperors of Rome, serving from 161 CE until his death in 180 CE. Living several centuries after Aristotle, this Roman ruler and field general centered his entire life around concepts of Stoicism. To be a Stoic is to be logical and moral, while to be a ruler is to sometimes sacrifice others in pursuit of a successful conquest. To be Aurelius was to rationally balance the good of the universe in slight favor against the good of his empire. He would consider questions like the ethics of exterminating all the men within a conquered city. Wouldn't it be better for the universe to leave a few males so that the city could eventually rebuild? Should a general exploit his environment by burning the enemy's crops and killing all his sheep?

If these ethical considerations by a general weren't unusual enough, he took the further step of creating a very descriptive diary, eventually codified in a book we read today as *Meditations*. In *Meditations*, Aurelius vividly describes his difficulties and sets forth his logic in making decisions. He admits he doesn't always make the ethical decision, yet he attempts to explain his failing by describing the anguish of being a leader. We are left to conclude this emperor viewed the entire world through a personal narrative centered around Stoic Ultrathoughts. *Meditations*, written nearly 1,900 years ago, is read as a preeminent work of literature, important to any person who seeks leadership.

Part III

CHAPTER 11

VARIOUS NATURES OF THE GODHEAD

As we move forward in review of the evolving nature of Ultra-thoughts on God and reality, it is important to clarify a key difference between the Greek/Hellenistic philosophers discussed and the next set of monotheistic philosophers/theologians. Pythagoras, Plato, Aristotle, and our Stoics conceptualized Godhead, God, or the gods in a generalized manner. As a result, their designs allowed for free consideration of a single God, many gods of various importance, a Godhead force, or any combination thereof. The specifics of the deity (or deities) were of little importance compared to the overall concept the philosopher attempted to describe. In fact, it is debatable whether my use of the word "specific" is even appropriate. If they only conceived of their Godhead, having never actually observed anything of substance, was there any physical characteristic needed at all?

The paradigm begins to change once a philosophy starts to mature, forming a foundation and attracting followers. When followers start to refine specific points of religion, the philosophy is urged to better define this holy presence. Is this force a specific God (monotheism), gods (polytheism) or a type of cosmic energy? Once those rudimentary specifics are agreed upon by people who subscribe to the philosophy, religious traditions and ceremonies can further develop, eventually resulting in a blend of religion and philosophy. Tradition and ceremony are tangible and physical experiences, not purely meta in nature. It is then expected that as a texture comes to surround the religion, the Godhead would tend to take on physical characteristics. The continued strength of religious dogma within the context of the broader society determines whether further refinement is allowed in the religion and or philosophy.

Stalwart monotheists today may find my words repulsive. They probably have a passionate belief that their God is a spiritual truth of the cosmos, not some tortuous theoretical concept of the Godhead. Nevertheless, this is a casual look at the history of Godhead philosophies. We're attempting to ultra-think, pushing our mind to its limits. We must free our mind of dogmatic preconceptions of God. If your God is truth, that God will survive our rather insignificant queries. Here I promote no particular notion, merely the freedom to consider a concept with unbiased clarity. If you find this book offensive, you probably shouldn't read the next: *Forbidden Philosophy*.

Followers of the dogma attached to a religion, believers in God, segregate themselves from the nonbelievers. Nonbelievers, those outside of the faith, are often referred to as atheists, pagans, or infidels. As dogma develops and traditions mature, societal members tend to stay together and form their own separate culture. To have a specific culture is by definition to exclude outsiders. Believers in a god become more segregated and over time continue to rely more on each other, which further binds the group. Liturgy and religious practice evolve within this specific culture creating a societal mind that has a particular tone in support of the society's preferred religion. Because of this customization, religion is often very difficult to export across culture without support of overt evangelism or outright conquest. The optimization of dogma within home culture creates a barrier to acceptance of foreign beliefs by outside cultures.

In this part of the book, we will consider the monotheistic concepts concerning the specific God of Abraham as described by Philo, Origen, Augustine, Plotinus, and Aquinas. Their theories or designs for God can seem muddled when evaluated by one not indoctrinated into a religion (Christianity) and the culture associated with this one version of God. With the exception of Philo, a Jewish philosopher, and Plotinus, a philosopher without any particular religion, the group can be described as Christian philosophers. They frequently delve into a concept known as the Holy Trinity of God or just the Trinity. The Trinitarian concept, which seems to imply three gods, is considered by these thinkers as synonymous with the One God of Abraham. At the earliest stage in the evolution of the religion of Christianity, there was probably no expectation that in order to evolve the Trinitarian concept in depth, it might be necessary to wrap back to the core philosophy and make some revisions.

Hearken back to our discussion of the use of statues by the ancients in the representation of gods. In a similar manner, Christian philosophy blends a spiritual God, a physical prophet, and a spiritual messenger. Any and each is the God of Abraham. This philosophy can become overwhelming to those unfamiliar with Christian monotheism and even for professed believers in the faith. As I understand it, and opinions do vary (please, don't write me in retort) the Trinitarian concept considers this One God of Abraham as being present in both the physical and spiritual realms at all points in time. God, often termed the Father, in concept also exists as Jesus (the Son), and a spiritual force that is a type of messenger or bridge between humans and God, known as the Holy Spirit. God may sometimes exist as material stuff but is principally represented as a spiritual entity.

The God of Abraham may have many names distinct by culture, yet regardless of the terminology used, philosophers who speak of this one God are always explicitly referring to the God who reputedly spoke to a man named Abraham. As documented by archaeologists, Abraham was a specific person, a tribal leader of sorts. It is believed he was born between 2500–2000 BCE. He resided in the southern portion of the Sumerian region of the Tigris and Euphrates River valley that today lies within modern day Iraq. According to traditions fundamental to the religions associated with Judaism, Christianity, and Islam, Abraham interacted with the one God, each making certain promises establishing a covenant or promise between God and the Jewish tribe of people. The people often simply referred to as "Jews" were a substantial community of people who, even to this day, maintain a culture distinct from others in the region.

Abraham is considered the patriarch of the original society and of all religions associated with the philosophy of this God. Despite disagreements surrounding the technicalities of liturgy and the fact that the surviving religions are not necessarily confined to members of the tribe, he is the same God for all three religions. The original God of Abraham religion, Judaism, remains to this day.

Roughly two thousand years after the advent of Judaism, a new religion evolved from the parent: the Christian religion. This religion elevates a specific Jewish prophet, Jesus, to the position of God personified, a Messiah (Savior). The religion purports that the appearance of this prophet was foretold by Judaism. Jesus thereby completes the Jewish chapter ushering in a new chapter in humanity. Jesus and God are basically if not exactly the same thing. But the religion went one step further: it added a third manifestation of the same God, the Holy Spirit. Such depth added would require a re-thinking of the original God concept. The Trinitarian concept was refined or simply added to what is often termed the "core philosophy" of Judaism. Naturally, believers in the Jewish religion reject this refinement.

Islam, another spin-off of Judaism, followed Christianity by about six to seven hundred years and doesn't include the concept of the Trinity. This religion updates and revises the original religion as it elevates the foretold appearance of the prophet Muhammad. The Prophet is viewed as God's chosen messenger. Quite similar to the prophet Moses dating back more than a thousand years, Muhammad is a God-guided reformer who corrects errors in the historical faith. The core philosophy of this religion has remained quite true to its parent. In a sense, Islam is closer to its Abrahamic roots than modern day Judaism. This religion still retains a concept of government within. In eons past, all three religions had incorporated some form of civil government, but today only Islam remains a classical theocracy. The religion still incorporates civil and spiritual laws in one system of overall belief.

Well over half of the world's population professes adherence to some variant of these Abrahamic religions. There are literally thousands of sects (subsets or communities) within these three specific religions. Regardless of sect or base religion, they all center around one God—whose philosophical roots we will now explore.

CHAPTER 12

PHILO

Philo of Alexandria (30 BCE–50 CE) was a Hellenized Jewish thinker, a monotheist who believed in one specific God—the God of Abraham. He grew up in the Egyptian city of Alexandria, at the time a part of the Roman Empire. The city's culture was dominated by the Greeks, and Philo was well versed in the ideas of Pythagoras, Plato, and Aristotle. He probably had access to remnants of, if not full volumes from the Library of Alexandria (burned and plundered decades before). This library was the greatest library of the ancient world having a reputed collection of nearly five hundred thousand works. Alexandria itself was a center of culture and history, with the library being among its most important structures. The focus of his ultra-thinking was the justification of his religion through a synthesis of Hellenistic philosophy and ancient religious texts of Judaism. To clearly understand his views, we must pause to define what the word *religion* meant to its Jewish followers.

Individuals who held to the tenets of Judaism during this era set themselves apart as a subset of Greco-Roman culture. Jews had managed to persuade the ruling political class of the Roman Empire to let them self-govern in no small degree. Over its history prior to Philo, nearly 2,500 years, a specific culture had developed around the Jewish philosophy and its religion. Provided Jews didn't flaunt their unique status in the empire, they were allowed to worship the One God of Abraham, maintain unusual dietary habits, and perform various spiritual rituals. They passively gave enough deference to the Roman sovereign to stay out of trouble with the rulers. They may have even acknowledged the Roman emperor as something like a god for the Roman people though he was not worthy of spiritual worship. Jews who lived near the Temple in Jerusalem, their official holy place that merged the physical and spiritual world of their God, were even allowed by the Romans to perform ritual animal sacrifices. Jews living in parts of the Diaspora (beyond a day's travel from the Jerusalem Temple) maintained their spiritual purity by observing the dogma promoted by religious leaders. Strict adherence, including memorizing religious teachings and celebrating sacred days, was required of a proper diasporic Jew like Philo.

Nevertheless, to stress merely the spiritual side of Judaism completely misses the mark when appreciating Philo as a philosopher. Judaism was a societal way of life with an unmatched legacy. To be a Jew meant to participate in a unique societal myth that had developed a distinct character. This society had developed legal concepts and rules of commerce, dress, eating, and courtship. Jewish teachers and spiritual leaders were magistrates to their flocks as much as the Roman authorities were. To fail to participate was to risk ostracization or outright removal from the group, and a Jew who left the protection of the group usually did not fare so well within the broader Roman society. The worship of God was certainly important, even central to society, but to be a Jew was to be a participant in a very rich cultural experience, a heritage of thousands of years.

As an essential member of the society, Philo was charged with using his intellect to enhance and interpret Judaism in his time, and in doing so he conceptualized an updated version of Plato's Ultrathoughts. He held Plato in reverence, calling him "most holy Plato," which leads some to characterize his work as merely a version of Platonism. But, unlike Plato, he had a very vivid interpretation of one specific God, which is why his philosophy seems more personal than most others of his era. Philo was a religious Jew who approached philosophy with his ideology intact. But make no mistake, he did manage to derive whole-brain Ultrathoughts that were very important. These ideas helped the religion evolve.

Philo's writings also bear a distinct Stoic character with their emphasis on morality. In merging various philosophies with Jewish interpretations of the God of Abraham, Philo refined the justification for the Jewish religion. Though he may not have intended it, upon reflection today it appears he provided a sound foundation for the Christian religion to come.

We are informed Philo read the Hebrew Bible, particularly the Torah (the first five books of the Bible), as allegory, allowing him a great deal of flexibility in reconciling the writings of Judaism with Hellenistic thought. For example, in the Genesis story, Adam and Eve were the original inhabitants of the earth, living in the Garden of Eden. To Philo, Adam represents not a physical human but the "mind" in metaphor; Eve represents the senses and animal nature of an individual. In considering another Biblical story—the story of Noah and his ark saving all the world's animals from the flood—the prophet Noah represented a metaphor for tranquility, a type of quiet confidence that God would provide a way. Going still deeper, Philo considered God not as a physical being with features but as a kind of spiritual omnipresence. The God of Abraham is beyond description as he lies outside of all matter. His version of God had little if any physical presence. This allowed the religion to free itself from the limitations of a specific geographic region surrounding the place of the Jewish Temple. Jews in the Diaspora were given support indirectly through this refinement of philosophy.

Philo continued and philosophized a new design: God did not create the stuff of the universe. God brought forth the perfect pattern of the ideal for all matter, but it was left to God's partner, the Logos or Word of God, to execute the actual organization of the material of the universe.

The theory of the Logos starts with God being both a kind of designer and presence. God is not the builder but the architect. From God emanated the builder, Logos, and each individual human soul. Since Logos and individual souls come from the God, each is pure and good. Still, they are clearly inferior to God.

Once Logos created all matter, the soul could exist on earth. The birth of a physical human child provides an earthly vessel for each human soul. Matter can never be pure because it doesn't come directly from God. The purity of any soul is contaminated from the moment it is partnered with the body. Note the similarity to Egyptian ideas.

In yet another consideration, Philo referred to the Bible's book of Genesis: God created man from dust (the material) and woman from man. The body of a human, however, has the fortune of attracting a soul. The soul, inherently good even if contaminated by its environment, nonetheless attempts to moderate the passions of an individual. Since people are subject to sensual desires and animal tendencies, they continually defile the character of their own soul. Philo maintained that this battle between the person and the soul is described in the Bible many times.

To be virtuous, individuals must resist physical pleasures and maintain self-control; the Platonian influence here becomes obvious. Individual actions determine the fate of the soul upon physical death. The particulars after death are not analyzed in depth by Philo. Unlike Plato, he was not inclined to consider the journey of the soul after death. At the death of the individual, only God would know the truth.

As a Jewish philosopher of prominence, could he have been familiar with a popular Jewish prophet, Jesus of Nazareth, who interacted with Jewish leadership for several years? Jews who viewed Jesus as unique among prophets (Christians, as they came to be called) were not excluded from Jewish society for at least one hundred years; therefore, Philo likely heard of the trouble caused by this nonconforming Jew. Just as a typical Jew did what was needed to satisfy Roman authorities, those who held religious opinions outside the mainstream simply kept their views to themselves. A Jew who followed Jesus likely did just enough to keep societal leaders appeased without compromising his or her spiritual integrity.

As we begin to ponder philosophers after Philo and his truly monumental theory of the Logos, we are left to consider whether he influenced the first Christian philosophers as well as the earliest followers of Jesus of Nazareth himself. We are reminded that Jesus was born and died during the height of Philo's popularity, so we might assume a discussion of Philo could have come up either with Jesus or his followers. And, although debate exists as to how widespread actual awareness of the prophet Jesus was during his lifetime, it is certain that Jesus drew the attention of Temple leaders to the point of even involving the Roman Empire itself—no insignificant matter. Philo may have been aware of this "troublemaker," Jesus.

Countless historians note that the concept of Logos has a certain harmony with Christian philosophy. Ultimately, acceptance of this new unique nature of God as being both a god as spirit and a man, by a very vocal minority of Jews would lead to a new religion: Christianity. When or how such a concept—the theology of the Christian God, the God of Abraham blended with a concept of the Trinity—was developed elicits strong opinion by believers. Religious dogma explains the entire process through active and overt action by the one God. Yet, at the time of the life of Jesus, some of his followers may have interpreted the teachings through a mind-myth that was already laced with the teachings of Hellenists or even specifically Philo.

Some theologians go so far as to assert that the authors of much of the Christian Bible (the Jewish Bible plus additional books in support of the Jesus story) were mimicking concepts developed by Philo. These scholars point to undeniable similarities between Logos and Jesus as the Messiah of the Christian faith. For instance, like the Logos, Jesus emanates from God and is something of a builder, playing an active and physical role in the interactive story of humanity and God.

To be clear, any notion of direct evidence of the influence of the Jew Philo on the first Christian apostles (early followers of Jesus who walked beside him) is speculative at best. Stalwart believers in the Christian faith find the very idea highly offensive if not subversive to their religion. However, it is not in dispute that Philo's ideas involving the Logos were considered, along with those of Plato and the ancient Egyptians, in the ultra-thinking of the first Christian philosophers who lived more than one hundred years after the passing of the man Jesus. From their Ultra-thoughts, the new religion, Christianity, would soon develop a unique dogma blending the physical and the spiritual in a manner never before seen in the history of humanity.

CHAPTER 13

ORIGEN

Living in Alexandria, Egypt near where Philo had lived two centuries earlier, Origen (184–253 CE) was one of the first philosophers to contemplate the life and reputed resurrection of the Jewish prophet Jesus. Origen eventually developed a philosophy of God that artfully incorporated both a spiritual and material reality. During this period, Christian beliefs were frequently viewed as simply variants of the Jewish religion, each tracing its roots to the philosophy of the One God of Abraham. Origen was not a Jew who later accepted Christian beliefs; he was one of the very earliest followers of what was becoming a distinct Christian religion. He joined one of the first schools of Christian theology at the age of eighteen, the Catechetical School of Alexandria founded by the apostle Mark.

As the child of a pagan father and Jewish mother who was a follower of Jesus, Origen was exposed to a variety of spiritual beliefs. He benefitted from his Alexandrian upbringing. Alexandria itself was a major port and sophisticated city situated at the mouth of the Nile River. It matured to be home to a massive collection of texts, many of which likely went back more than four thousand years. Although history tells us that much of the Alexandrian Library collection had been destroyed by the army of Julius Caesar in 48 BCE, a substantial number of scrolls and books remained in or around the city until roughly 400 CE.

The cosmopolitan city was well known as a place of violence and persecution throughout the life of Origen. As an adolescent, he witnessed the martyrdom of many Christians, including some of his own kin, at the hands of the Romans. While in general, Jewish society still remained privileged within Roman society during the time of Origen, the Christian subset of Jews were outliers and frequently the target of persecution for a variety of reasons—not the least of which is they sought to convert underprivileged Roman citizens to their fledgling belief system. Origen felt a bond with those individuals and is said to have idealized thoughts of martyrdom himself in defense of the right of any person to seek their true faith. Growing to maturity and valuing his own freedom of belief, he often fasted and generally followed an ascetic lifestyle.

Although Origen was immersed in the teachings of the catechetical school, he was not a model student. In fact, we might say that Origen flunked out of Christian divinity school. He evidently didn't agree with many of the positions espoused by his quasi-Jewish elders. Having been banished from the catechetical school, he traveled extensively. Ultimately, he found himself in Palestine, where he eventually started his own school in Caesarea built on a foundation of Aristotelian logic and the Socratic method. Palestine, the actual region where Jesus walked and taught, came to be home to the Library of Caesarea, a rich collection of early Christian writings. Using these sources, Origen came to be in a unique position, one of synthesizing some of the earliest and most complete authentic Christian philosophy without the drag of either Jewish or Christian tradition.

During this time, be reminded that Christianity to most was simply another variation of Judaism; nevertheless, it was becoming obvious to Jesus followers that its uniqueness demanded a more lucid design. To create this modified blueprint of Godhead design, Christianity would need to formally and overtly break from Judaism. To break from the Jews, Christians had no choice but to shed significant parts of established Jewish tradition. Origen had never been a traditional Jew and had no special reverence for its traditions. He was free to ultra-think the meaning of this person, Jesus, who was said to have been resurrected. This allowed him to harmonize Jesus with God separately and distinctly from other Jewish prophets. Once Origen came to understand that this physical person was actually the One God of Abraham in the flesh, he freshly considered the philosophical implications from not a Jewish but a Hellenistic lens created through a keen understanding of Greek philosophy.

Christian philosophy is unique in that it incorporates not only the metaphysical concept of God and soul but also a material man, Jesus. Jesus—a recognized prophet, teacher, and miracle worker amongst the Jewish people—had been crucified by the Romans at the behest of Jewish Temple leadership in 31–34 CE. Pursuant to the Christian view, God performed a miracle when he resurrected the man Jesus from death. The all-powerful God expressed love for humanity by allowing the sacrifice of himself (or the Son, Jesus, as represented in Christian dogma) through means of crucifixion. But, in living testament to the power of God, Jesus in physical presence lived and walked again amongst witnesses. This event thereby cemented an updated version of the story of the One God of Abraham as told by the Jews. Jesus, a resurrected man, is Christ the Messiah, the Savior of all humanity pursuant to the belief. Jesus is now God, and God, Jesus.

To "believe in Jesus" one is having faith in the general description of this philosophy and/or associated sectarian Christian dogma. Christian religious dogma as promoted by various sects (denominations) put forth nuance to this general philosophy that describes the story of the humanity of Jesus, his teachings, and miracles. Specific events associated with the prophet Jesus were seen as a fulfillment of the Jewish prophecy referenced in ancient texts that had already been adapted to Jewish tradition.

As individuals ruminated on the Christian philosophy and Jewish religious tradition, they further refined, framed, and put forth their own interpretations. The popularity of these interpretations ebbed and flowed. As the story of Jesus aged, it needed to make an overt break from Judaism. Origen lived near the precipice of this break. He proved instrumental in refining the monotheistic philosophy associated with Jewish religion in a manner agreeable to Christians. Ultimately, the core philosophy concerning the One God of Abraham matured to become a Trinitarian philosophy in Christian lore. Over the coming decades, its further maturation would allow for two distinct dogmas: that which continues to support the Jewish religion and one that supports the newer Christian religion.

Today, Christians look at the One God of Abraham philosophy of the Jews as a raw and foundational version of their specific Trinitarian philosophy. I suggest Christian concepts harmozine at least as much with ideas described by Plato as those of the Jews. Origen, along with others of his day, seems to have blended a lucid expression of a Judeo-Christian and the tripartite described by Plato. In doing so he legitimized Christianity as a worthy standalone philosophy separate and apart from that of the Jews. He is cited as a source by virtually every early Christian theologian.

Remarkably, today most Christian theologians, priests, and pastors of Europe and the Americas barely reference Origen. They shun his ideas in favor of the later philosopher Augustine, but it is Origen's earlier interpretation of Christian philosophy that dominates Christian theology in the Eastern church. As the religion matured and evolved, eventually the philosophy of Origen became a forbidden philosophy as far as the Western church was concerned. Apparently, his views came to be seen as being simply too philosophical in nature. To emphasize the philosophy indirectly slighted the actual religion.

In considering Origen, we are confident that for him God is an eternal being outside time and space. Yet, as Origen espouses his philosophy, he moves forward to describe God as being in Heaven. This opens the door to confusion. Is God, the Father, for Origen truly meta or is he also a physical being like Jesus? The commonly accepted manner of interpreting Origen is to view his philosophy as interpreting God as equally physical and spiritual. I say "accepted manner" to allude to the schism between Eastern and Western Christians. Considering Jesus, however, it appears Origen interpreted Jesus as somewhat more physical than spiritual.

As the Christian religion evolved, it would face a major challenge some hundreds of years after the death of Origen. The Great Schism, or the splitting of the Christian faith into camps of east (Eastern Orthodox) and west (Roman Catholic), can be traced to one specific controversy: the question of whether Jesus and the Holy Spirit are the exact same being as the one true God of Abraham or not. The issue has dire philosophical implications for the idea of the Holy Trinity—three God concepts merged into one God. What is the exact nature of each component? Are they one and the same, or are they each a separate manifest presence unified in purpose? This question must be fully answered in order for the religion to be adequately defended. Agreement would not be found and the Christian religion started to split. As parties became more vocal in dissent, differences in philosophy became entangled with ongoing political disputes, leading to an overt and official split in 1054. After this date, there were two principal variants of Christian thought. Each embraced the broad idea of the Holy Trinity (core to Christianity) but the differences in details were significant enough that religious war ensued.

Let's refocus the discussion to the philosophy of Origen. Like so many of his era, he built his Ultrathoughts with Plato in mind. He then naturally emphasized the nonmaterial, the spiritual, in his concepts. Still, when he was forced to consider Jesus, he knew this person walked and lived a physical existence. In his ultra-thinking, he had no choice but to place Jesus in the physical realm. Logically Origen knew the physical realm couldn't be pure, and God, being pure, must be beyond physical matter. Whether intentional or not, these musings left him to imply, if not outright say, Jesus must be just slightly less than God.

That Ultrathought, the Trinity, would prove to be problematic for the religion. It is a hard concept to wrap your mind around and has been a challenge for those who have seriously contemplated the Christian version of the Godhead. Did Origen succeed and adequately ultra-think the concept of the Trinity? Even the very first Christians, those who may have literally seen a mortal man die and walk again, couldn't seem to explain it to the satisfaction of all, so if Origen misses his mark, he's in good company.

Setting the Trinity aside for the moment, in possibly his best writing Origen defines the nature of God through logic. He spells out very specific justifications in advocacy of a belief in the Christian version of the God of Abraham. Through his seminal work, *On the First Principles*, he stands with Augustine and Aquinas among the greatest of the Christian apologists. Less than two hundred years after the death of Jesus he proves the Christian faith worthy of becoming a world religion. His Ultrathoughts evaluate literal versus metaphorical interpretations of Christian and earlier Hebrew texts as well as how each relates to a believer in the faith. He undoubtedly had access to some of the earliest Christian writings, which brought a significant deal of depth to his thought.

Christian philosophy is obviously similar to that of both Plato and Philo the Jewish philosopher. With regards to Philo and his description of the Logos, we note Jesus comes from God just as Logos comes from God. But be reminded that Jesus and the Holy Spirit don't merely emanate from the Godhead—they are the God(s) of the Trinity. The principle reason this becomes critically important to Christian dogma and liturgy lies in how believers or followers are to worship their God. The New Testament, the Christian addition to the Jewish holy book, clearly states believers are to worship Jesus as the one true God. Logos, per Philo, is never God and deserves no worship in the Jewish religion.

Of course, when considering any religion or spiritual faith, all spiritual dogma falls apart under objective comparison to the beliefs of another or the rigor of scientific evaluation. That is the core difference between faith and science. At some point, one must simply admit he or she is willing to have faith, a belief, without serious hope of objective proof.

CHAPTER 14

PLOTINUS

P lotinus (205–270 CE) was born in lower Egypt. He was most likely of Roman or Hellenized Egyptian heritage. Though he was from a family of some status, he had grown weary of materialism by his late twenties and became attracted to the philosophy of Plato. Known as a bit of an eccentric, he eventually devoted his life to contemplation, pure philosophy. At the age of thirty-eight, after considering many Ultrathoughts, including Eastern philosophies dealing with concepts of the world soul, he curiously joined the Roman army. Unfortunately, he was abandoned behind enemy lines in Persia. As an artful and persuasive speaker, he managed to talk his way out of the region and found his way back to Rome where he thoroughly developed his design.

The One, the Intellect, and the Soul, as described by Plotinus (circa 250 CE) in *The Enneads*, are to this day considered among the most refined design used to relate God and humanity in the spiritual. Being first grounded in the ideas of Plato, his evolved Ultrathoughts came to be called Neoplatonism. The One could be viewed as analogous to the universe of all, inclusive of the Godhead. The presence is transcendent, timeless, and is all that is or ever will be. The One can't be described as good, eternal, self-aware, or anything specifically. The One is all attributes at once. Conceptually superior to the concept of a world soul and completely foreign to most modern monotheistic impressions of God, the One simply *is*. In describing the One, Plotinus represents an analogy of light, the Divine Intellect, or the sun. Caution must be used when describing the One. In our human terms of language, technically the One is beyond description in terms of attributes. The One was not created. It is nothing and everything at the same time.

From the One, Plotinus tells us the Intellect (a.k.a. the Nous or the Mind) emanated, and, from this second level a third emanates, the Soul. The Soul is then split between the upper soul and lower soul. The lower would be analogous to the individual human soul, while the upper would be a collective or world soul in concept. The lower level, or human soul, has the unique privilege of interacting with the physical; the upper does not. The Intellect maintains wisdom and understanding, having good sense. Aristotle's influence on Plotinus appears obvious as the philosopher systematically describes the virtue to be gained through the pursuit of contemplation, logic, and understanding.

The Intellect, as the source of all souls, directly provides the individual with the instinct necessary to do that which is wise. Note the two types of soul, world and lower (human) soul, are not directly connected to the One. Soul is not of the One, but of the Intellect. The Intellect is sometimes described as a kind of cosmic mind that blesses souls with a slice of innate wisdom.

The physical human, though partnered with lower soul, is subject to animal desires. People are animals that are blessed with a lower soul. The soul remains in a constant battle for dominance with the individual throughout the partnership. At death, the human soul is reincarnated into another physical body. The lower soul inherently needs a partner.

This Neoplatonic view has been incorporated into countless religious beliefs with various modifications. Plotinus was likely among the first to describe it in or around the Mediterranean Basin, but it has many variations. When historians debate the roots of various religions, there often exists vigorous discussion about whether a specific philosophical concept was developed before, in parallel with, or after the writings of Plotinus. Neoplatonism has a very similar ring to several incredibly old philosophies, including those of ancient Egypt, Sumer, and even pre-European America.

I suggest that very few ideas are original; consequently, it's safe to assume that the concept of an eternal Godhead complete with world soul and human soul doesn't merely exist because of the thoughts of specific philosophers named Plato and Plotinus. Concepts of God and soul may be part of the makeup of our species. Though philosophers like Plotinus may have been among the best at expressing their Ultrathoughts, it is doubtful they fully deserve their reputation for originality.

With that said, there is no doubt Plotinus was a brilliant philosopher. He absolutely deserves credit for taking the time to write *The Enneads*, a seminal work written over a period of several years. This book represents a consolidation of his Ultrathoughts throughout his lifetime, not simply his concept of the One. He and his editor, Porphyry, provide some very refined descriptions of his Godhead design written in a readable manner that has been sourced by hundreds of thousands of individuals over the centuries. The example of Plotinus should serve as an example of what the mind can do. To think is good for humanity.

CHAPTER 15

AUGUSTINE

Though there are various versions of its core beliefs, the single most popular religion in the world is Christianity. Roughly one-third of the world's population as of 2012 define themselves as being Christian. Despite his later-life conversion one philosopher, Augustine of Hippo (354–430 CE), has done more to build that congregation than any other.

While philosophies of God don't dictate who can subscribe to the philosophy, religions often do. As a philosophy morphs into a religious dogma it tends to dictate life's winners and losers. Most religions determine membership by privilege of birth. People are born into a religion. There are exceptions of course, and various religions do allow newcomers provided some type of "payment" is made in return. That cost could be material sacrifice, actual payment of money or goods, a benefit of marriage into a chosen family, or acquisition of social status. Membership in most religions is a privilege to be earned or passed down. Perhaps this is best represented by precise dogma associated with Judaism and Hinduism. Each very specifically documents why some persons are to be given a privilege before the Godhead.

At its origin, a unique aspect of the Christian philosophy associated with the story of Jesus was his outreach to the unwashed masses. Nonbelievers were encouraged to consider membership for themselves. Though its parent religion, Judaism, defines privilege by birth, the prophet Jesus shunned the idea. In doing so, he laid the foundation for a modified version of religion overall. The action by Jesus as the Son of God made payment for any and all persons. This new Christian model made it very clear that Jesus (a.k.a. God) accepts converts regardless of social class, birth, or payment. Faith is the required "payment," a simple affirmation of belief.

Jesus himself provided the conduit for acceptance of individuals who weren't historically considered worthy by the Jewish religion. In becoming human, dying, and living again, God through His alternative physical presence, Jesus, paid the price of admission of humanity into the heretofore privileged realm. No further material sacrifice was necessary by any prospective convert. This fundamentally promotes later-life conversion by any person who chooses to subscribe to the system of belief. It also implicitly disparages any and all privileges of birth, wealth, and societal status.

This back-handed slap to authority and aristocracy has played a large part in the persecution of believers. Such disparagement of birthright privilege and disrespect of caste overall assures believers that God, not humans, is in control. Christianity specifically places the poor on level with the elite. As the religion became more popular, leaders took note and constantly needed to take action to keep the masses in line, otherwise authority itself would be put at risk. You may note this is a fundamental reason that this religion frequently conflicts with forms of authoritative government.

Augustine, living in the region of modern-day Algeria in northern Africa, grew up in a family that had a history of Roman support. This earned him Roman privilege and possibly even citizenship. As a young man, Augustine traveled extensively and was highly educated by prestigious thinkers of his day. Though he himself had been privileged, his inquiring mind and philosophical training led him to spend many of his formative years searching for life's meaning throughout the Mediterranean basin. There can be no doubt that he was consumed by Ultrathoughts. Like so many of the greatest philosophical thinkers, he eventually became so disillusioned through these experiences that he resigned himself to leading a life of asceticism and contemplation.

Despite efforts to remove himself from society, he kept coming back to study peculiarities of the Christian faith. The prophet Jesus was well schooled in his religion, Judaism, and undoubtedly knew his Torah extremely well. Augustine noted how particularly attracted Jesus was to the idea of "brotherly" love. This type of love was eloquently described by the Jewish religious leader Hillel the Elder (circa 30 BCE). Hillel, in reading the very same Jewish Torah, noted a principle point of the holy writing could be reduced to a rather simple appreciation: every person is of equal value to God. Therefore, a worthy gauge of the quality of an action put upon another is to reverse your circumstance. Today we call this the Golden Rule that Christians tend to paraphrase as: do unto others as you would have them do unto you. Many if not most teachings of Jesus seemed to revolve around this central concept, according to Augustine. This emphasis on love lay in direct opposition to the Neoplatonic focus on the intellect and the naturalist view that all is material. Augustine noticed his ultra-thinking seemed to harmonize best with ideas of Jesus.

Though it had been nearly four hundred years since the reputed resurrection of Jesus, Christianity as a religion was still in its infancy at this time. Exactly like Origen decades before, Augustine's mother was a follower of Jesus, but he wasn't. There were many flavors of Christianity being controlled by leaders serving various local flocks. Although there was a weak standardized dogma, various local pockets were starting to develop unique Christian traditions. Nevertheless, many of the basics we understand today as "Christianity" hadn't been universally accepted. Some scholars would go so far as to say that during Augustine's time only a minority of Christians believed in the resurrection of the physical body of Jesus.

Today we take for granted that any Trinitarian concept must involve an actual resurrection of the man, yet technically that is not necessary. The concept at its base simply means three as one: God of Abraham, Jesus, and Holy Spirit (a.k.a. Father, Son, and Holy Spirit). Jesus could be God or a Godhead component without literally walking and talking as a physical being after death. Physical resurrection may be a key facet of the religion, but it is not of the philosophy. This view is foreign today, but it was not unique many hundreds of years ago. In the context of philosophy, nothing can bind or restrict God. Resurrection, therefore, would not be absolutely necessary. What did Augustine believe? We can't be absolutely sure. He was a philosopher who was oriented toward meta ideas and philosophers are notoriously hard to pin down. Still, his writings do seem to lean into the idea that the physical man did, in fact, walk and talk after death. Frankly, my personal view is that he would shrug his shoulders at the very question. Like most in his era, he was all about the message, not the details.

Augustine was an unusually prolific man, writing hundreds of works or letters, many of which proved instrumental in establishing church doctrine. Augustine clarified the procedures and purpose of the Christian sacraments (ceremonies) that eventually formed a sort of guide for clergy. To this day many of these same procedures are still in use throughout all three major subsets of the Christian religion: Roman Catholic, Eastern Orthodox, Protestant.

He used ultra-thinking as he meditated on the most ancient Jewish and Christian texts in circulation through the lens of his Hellenistic view. Serving as the bishop (senior member of the church) of Hippo for decades, his theological musings on these documents were copied and disseminated to dozens of Christian churches. Since he served so long, wrote so well, and was located in a port city, his specific Ultrathoughts began to overwhelm alternative interpretations of the faith. The city of Hippo, a principle Mediterranean port, became a hub of information for collecting, reviewing, and standardizing all Christian doctrine. The religion was growing rapidly and needed guidance from someone like Augustine to solidify traditions. Senior believers naturally looked to Augustine, a renowned expert in the faith, to train new members of the clergy.

One of the more interesting facts surrounding Augustine is that he was instrumental in creating our common and very visual interpretation of the physical places known as Heaven and Hell. For him to be credited with such tangible aspects of the religion is ironic because his personal interpretations were likely far more allegorical than literal. In fact, it is debatable as to whether he actually believed in something as tangible as a physical resurrection.

Coming to his belief in his thirties, Augustine stated that he accepted the Christian faith only after his appreciation of the allegory represented in the teachings of Jesus. It is commonly accepted that he would have read the earliest Christian texts, some possibly written by the hand of an apostle. It seems he thought as a Hellenist, so he wouldn't have hesitated to read from alternative sources like Egyptian funerary texts. Given this meta orientation, for him to be credited with solidifying Christian perceptions of a literal physical God sitting on his throne in Heaven is a bit strange.

In his era, Augustine was writing hundreds of letters to people across a broad region. We can assume some of those churches had members who spoke various languages. I surmise that some nuance regarding what was meant to be taken as allegory versus literal was lost in translation. Of course, he can't be solely credited with these literal interpretations of biblical writings; artwork by master painters such as Michelangelo have done their part to bind certain images to the Christian faith. Still, many would be forced to admit that if the literal images so fundamental to Christianity were invented by people rather than by God, it was Augustine who did it best.

Many of the images that became an integral part of the texture of the Christian religion can be traced to one particular set of his writings: *City of God*. Although the work itself may not have been popularized until hundreds of years after the death of Augustine, *City of God* reads like a theatrical production representing official Christian dogma to this day. The work is the result of his ultra-thinking during a time when the Roman Empire was falling again, this time for good.

Over a period of years, he wrote a series of philosophical works in which he likened Rome to the kingdom of Satan being punished by God—Satan, of course, being a presence or entity that seduces humans to act against the will of God. The Christian church is presented as the advocate of God being victimized by Rome. God versus Satan, allegorically presented as church versus Rome.

During this period, Christians were being blamed by laypeople for the fall of the Empire. Consequently, it is very likely that in defense of his flock Augustine wanted to refocus the blame on Satan and the Roman government. In the writing, the realm of Satan had its leader—the Devil, God's adversary. Since Rome was on land and Hell was below, the Devil ruled a vibrant underworld complete with neverending tumult and endless fiery pain. To match the very physical Devil, God also took on a physical presence. He was presented as sitting at a throne in a place in the clouds called Heaven, complete with pearly gates, angels, and rejuvenated humans who had been resurrected to reside in the permanent bliss above. Over several years, Augustine explored concepts of good and evil in vivid detail through this type of writing. Heaven and the underworld of Satan came to life. Through his use of allegory, Augustine brightly described the literal battles within the Empire as intertwined with the spiritual battle faced by the soul of man. This spiritual war manifested itself on earth through the fall of the Roman Empire.

As the number of Christian followers grew and became widely dispersed within various cultures the stories of Augustine continued to resonate. Many only knew of Christianity through his writings. In his era Christian Bibles didn't exist in any meaningful sense. To know of the religion was to hear of the religion as a story told by a leader. That leader was probably instructed by the Ultrathoughts of "Saint" Augustine.

Within decades of the passing of Augustine, the religion became more removed from its foundational source religion, Judaism, and the common individual had no information concerning the actual philosophy behind the Christian religion. As *City of God* became disassociated further from its context as well, the stories of Augustine formed a kind of philosophical foundation for Christianity. For thousands if not millions, knowledge of the religion was first obtained by hearing of these allegorical scenes from *City of God*. Religious doctrine grew organically, and with this texture as background, I ultra-think church leaders eventually did not attempt to distinguish the literal from the allegorical within the belief. Like the Christian believers in general, many members of the clergy were probably not sophisticated enough to understand the nuances of Augustine's allegory.

One of the more in-depth philosophical interpretations of Augustine are his Ultrathoughts regarding his view of the nature of the soul. To understand his view of the soul one should compare his Ultrathoughts to Neoplatonism. In the Augustinian view, there is no world soul, and animals (other than people) have no soul. The soul follows a path. The soul begins at its cohabitation with the human body as an imperfect image of the timeless God of Abraham, not the perfect image, Jesus. The Augustinian version of the human soul always seeks to be near God, the Father.

The key point here is "near God," not "reunited with God" or reincarnated. Once free from the physical body at death, the path of a successful journey of the soul is provided through grace (a gift of acceptance) offered by God. An unsuccessful journey (rejection of acceptance by God) doesn't lead to reincarnation—there is no second chance. The visual of a believer kneeling before God or Jesus is an image that comes to mind. A successful soul resides for eternity near God in Heaven, while a failed soul resides for eternity in Hell. The soul has but one physical human partner in all eternity.

In the Christian philosophy as expressed by Augustine, neither the individual nor the church can obligate God to do anything with regards to the afterlife. The soul may sit with God only through the grace of God. A person can be as God-like or more appropriately "Jesus-like" as possible, but at the passing of the physical body, no one can obligate God to act. The church is important to people because God deemed it so, however, God alone decides the winners and losers. Pursuant to his Ultrathoughts based on his reading and prayerful meditation, Augustine states that no soul can ever truly be worthy of God. This idea likely stems from the fact that since the soul remains only an imperfect image of God, the soul will always fall short of God's perfection. Grace (a gift of forgiveness, since no soul is worthy) is necessary for a fulfilled journey of the soul.

Further, Augustine reminds us that individuals can always seek to improve themselves in the eyes of God, but this can only be done through imitation of the perfect image of God—Jesus the Son. Humans are an imperfect image. Jesus, even as a man, remains the only perfect image. Key to the philosophy is to stress that this Son should not be thought of as any less than God the Father. To believe and follow Jesus Christ is not an intellectual pursuit, understanding, or the exercising of ritual, but fully an exercise in faith. The faith declares that as individuals seek God through the imitation of Jesus, God will ultimately deem them worthy of a "seat" near his presence upon the passing of the physical body.

An individual's only worthy action involves honoring God, and mimicry of the life of Jesus as he resided on earth for a brief period. The mimicry might be said to boil down to "Love everyone as you would your child, and maintain the utmost humility and deference to God the creator of all." You will note the philosophy's similarity to both Stoicism and various Eastern philosophies. The motto could have been written by both Marcus Aurelius or Confucius without much forethought. But once Augustine is fully understood you will note a very important distinction unique to Christian philosophy, personal humility.

Let's contrast this Christian idea that humility is important with those of Stoicism. In the view of a Stoic, living a good life builds confidence in people, and such confidence is good. For Christian followers living a good life is desirable, but unchecked personal confidence is bad.

In Christian theology, the process flows as follows: confidence builds the individual ego, which in turn results in pride and boasting. This tends to make individuals reluctant to humble themselves before God. Humility is difficult to maintain as self-confidence increases. Humility before God is an overarching facet of the faith. Therefore, pride and lack of humility are the principal reasons for the failure of a soul as judged before God. God alone grants grace to the soul. But if the person is too prideful to worship God, they might not want to count on grace being granted. This knowledge has been passed down through sacred texts for thousands of years, so Christians are instructed to seek success, but not so much that the believer becomes prideful. You may note that although Christianity may first appear shallow—a belief in the resurrection of a man who is also God—a full understanding of the theology brings forth the nuance and complexity of the concept. An individual must artfully live in a world of physical distractions all the while imitating Jesus and not accepting any hint of credit for their efforts.

The ultra-thinking of Augustine led him to conclude that regardless of the level of success attained by an individual in his or her attempt to mimic Jesus Christ, the effort must be sincere. Faith in the process is far more important than success in the attempt. He states that when the follower struggles but nevertheless strives diligently, the believer shall gain confidence pleasing to God. Confidence is not assurance, of course; therefore, the Christian should not gain pride through any individual effort. Humanity must always remain humble since grace—forgiveness of one who is not worthy—is the exclusive right of God. But "Faith will not disappoint" is the teaching taken from the Bible, so faith in the process is all a believer will ever have.

This summarizes Augustine's philosophy of God and God's relationship to man, which is, theoretically, mainstream Christian design today. These concepts stress the spiritual nature of God and a person's purely metaphysical God-experience. The irony is that as the church embraced the interpretations of Augustine to build a religious dogma in support of Christian philosophy, it eventually lost sight of his use of allegory. I suggest that his philosophy was so full of texture that what was conceived in allegory eventually came to represent itself in religious dogma as a set of very literal beliefs.

This very literal interpretation eventually became the primary blueprint of the religion. As traditions of the Christian church evolved several hundred years post-Augustine, official doctrine left very little doubt: the Christian version of the ancient texts were free of error, God often manifested himself physically, the Devil was a physical being, Heaven and Hell are physical places. A spiritual work of philosophy morphed into a literal truth. To believe otherwise was blasphemous, against the official opinion of the church. This literal interpretation became the dominant way to think of the religion. This would soon present a major problem for the religion in a world dominated by science.

Part IV

CHAPTER 16

THOMAS AQUINAS: THE DEFENDER

Thomas Aquinas from the province of Frosinone near Naples, Italy, didn't live to see his fiftieth birthday. Aquinas was a Christian who some believe was literally put on this earth by God for one reason: to save the Christian religion. In retrospect, he did save the religion from becoming an antiquated belief defended solely by the force of tradition and dogma, regardless of whether that task was or wasn't preordained by God himself.

A Dominican friar of the Roman Catholic sect, he came to prominence circa 1260 CE during a time when the truth of religion—any religion—was being reconsidered. Over the years, Christian traditions sanctioned by church leaders had evolved to promote a very literal interpretation of the faith. As time passed this caused the religion to take on an almost mythological characterization. Believers were told of literal angels, pearly gates of Heaven, water turning into wine, etc. Furthermore, the religion had bound itself to state governance. This meant traditions of church were interwoven with and often couldn't be separated from the ruling aristocracy themselves.

As university education became more common in Europe, Aristotelian logic began to fascinate the mind of the influential elite class. For years these formally educated citizens had held firm in their support of authorized dogma promoted by both church and state. Eventually, angst began to build, and it became difficult in social circles to support positions held by the church that the educated class saw as illogical or unscientific. Science simply makes sense to an educated person actively seeking objective proof in support of one's beliefs.

Requesting proof of the validity of religious sacraments would soon be considered not only sound but necessary if one was to be educated and support a spiritual religion. At first only a few openly questioned the truth of religious sacraments (ceremonial practices that often purport a metaphysical truth), but over time the number of inquiring minds grew. Of course, church sacraments that emphasize principles like the literal manifestation of the blood of Christ from wine or holy water blessed by a priest lie outside the proof of science. We realize this today, but in the Middle Ages what could or couldn't be proven by scientific rigor was not so clear-cut. Smart people with no inherent desire to destroy their faith were asking sincere questions. The scientific method was being applied to religious rituals purporting to have some sort of influence on God, man, or material reality. This pressure of science against Christian dogma put the two on a collision course. Being one of the Catholic's best and brightest, Aquinas created Ultrathoughts to provide cover for the church, and in doing so, he also protected the ruling government. Through his Ultrathoughts, he eloquently blended existing Christian principles and the logic of Aristotle.

Complicating this challenge was that during this time Islam, a faith centered around the same God but without recognition of Jesus as Savior, was rapidly expanding worldwide. One of the reasons for the success of Islam was that over a couple of hundred years, a time when the Christian religion was stagnating under a series of "Bad Popes," Islam was modernizing. The Middle East, the traditional home of Islam, was in the midst of an Islamic Golden Age. This was a time when thinkers invented hundreds of things, from the toothbrush to algebra. Islam embraced the wisdom of the ancient Greeks and was not bound to the literal interpretation of dogma. Their religion seemed to hold the high ground regarding logic and science. Christianity, on the other hand, had grown to fear change and fell back on the defense of tradition as a strategy to maintain its dominance in the minds of believers. Since the Muslims, followers of the faith of Islam, had co-opted the logic of Aristotle, the foes—science and Islam—appeared united in their opposition to Christianity. From the standpoint of the Christian church, any endorsement of science was a capitulation to the Muslim threat, but Aquinas discovered a work-around through his Ultrathoughts.

Although trained by the church, in a practical sense Aquinas appears today as a philosopher first. During his lifetime, a period following the Dark Age of Europe, he was a philosopher with few equals. Like any person of the church who dared to consider the pagan philosophy of Hellenists, he initially met significant resistance to his ideas. Though he was trying to help the church, many church leaders condemned the Ultrathoughts of Aquinas and even advocated his excommunication from the fold—particularly those from Paris who had their own internal drama with the Romans. In their minds, he was not a follower of the faith, and he clearly proved their point in his advocacy of thinkers like Aristotle. Nevertheless, despite a sometimes-rocky beginning, Aquinas eventually prevailed to become a saint in Christian lore.

Looking at his accomplishments, today we may be inclined to say his task was nothing special. Yet once we appreciate that during his era anyone who even dared to openly discuss a view contrary to accepted beliefs could literally be tortured to death, we can begin to recognize what he meant to the religion.

Considering his twist on Christian philosophy in relation to Greek thought, he stated that fundamentally God provides all, including all knowledge—a statement in agreement with Aristotle. This perfect knowledge is available directly to humanity—without a human mediator—through God via the Holy Spirit. The Holy Spirit is a uniquely Christian concept that the faith of Islam lacks. Physical persons are considered flawed. Perfect knowledge is only provided through God. However, humanity may be too dull to comprehend such perfection.

This is where the logic of Aquinas comes in to prove that Christianity lives in harmony with the ideas of Aristotle: God provides perfect scientific knowledge to man. Since the church of the Christian faith advocates for God, the Christian church is an advocate of science—not an enemy of scientific thought.

Aquinas preferred more general and philosophical discussions. He attempted to avoid specific issues surrounding the application of the scientific method. When urged to get involved in such details, he clarified his basic assumption. Even if apparent contradictions arose that seemed to imply the church was in error, this represented a simple failure of human comprehension. Wrong conclusions are expected of the foolish; therefore, the church and God are always in agreement even if we don't understand how. Aquinas consistently focused on logic and, likely for his own self-preservation, did his best not to get into specifics.

Being well versed in many philosophical theories, Aquinas systematically reinterpreted the Ultrathoughts of several Hellenistic thinkers whose opinions were held in high esteem by the educated class. He absorbed virtually every concept of the soul and God and adapted them to generally accepted Christian dogma. The science of Aristotle and his detailed descriptions of biological life, highlighting the beauty of nature, per Aquinas directly supports the primacy of a perfect God, since natural symmetry and beauty prove the influence of God.

Among the many writings of Aquinas, the *Summa Theologica* stands out. This work explains the wonders of God himself as Aquinas methodically builds a narrative in support of Christian theology. Through an Aristotelian style, the style of a scientist, he uses logic to demonstrate the existence of God. This same logic in support of God is still used today. The *Summa Theologica* gives intellectuals the credibility they seek to not only defend their beliefs but bring forth sound arguments used to refute nonbelievers through a refined philosophy of God.

Aristotle wrapped many of his rational arguments within the context of good and evil. Coming from the Platonist school and its reverence for asceticism, he considered material aspects to be secondary and ultimately evil. In the view of Aquinas, these concepts could be used directly to bolster the Christian position that tied Satan to the material world. That is precisely what Aquinas did with unmatched skill. He used his anti-materialist Ultrathoughts, built on the writings of Augustine, to develop the idea that to be Christlike is to be fair and honest and to offer your products at a reasonable price. Both Christ and Aristotle presented an anti-materialist stance, where money and all other physical stuff should be avoided. Representing the physical as fundamentally evil may not be that impressive; others had done the same. However, Aquinas expands the concept and observes that since the immaterial spiritual soul uses the physical body— not the other way around—it proves the superiority of the soul provided by God. God can never lose to the evil realm dominated by Satan, that which both Aquinas and Aristotle considered the physical realm.

Aquinas appreciated science and the intellect, but he did not believe all would be known. Who can know the mind of the perfect immaterial God? Any notion that science was near equal or superior to God would not stand. While science is fine, and knowledge is good for man's soul, the idea of the equality of science and God was blasphemy pursuant to his ultra-thinking. Furthermore, such a representation shows the evil nature of anyone who would think such a thing. His brilliant synthesis of thought, which blended worthy Ultrathoughts from the giants of philosophy and his deeply held Christian beliefs, allowed science to be considered by the Christian believer in a manner that showed deference to both church and state.

CHAPTER 17

GOD VERSUS SCIENCE

While Thomas Aquinas and his Ultrathoughts provided an adequate defense of Christian religion for a few hundred years, eventually all spiritual beliefs—regardless of the religion—would face the wrath of those armed with the scientific method. A critical battle in this ongoing war between those who demand objective proof and those who can't quite prove anything can be traced to the 15th century, a period when Europe came to adopt movable type printing technology.

The rigor of scientific critique is fundamental to the building of quality science. The wider dissemination of scientific research as a result of the adoption of inexpensive printing meant more analysis and review. More scientific rigor demanded that still more information be grounded in the methodology. The quantity and quality of scientific knowledge exploded within two hundred years of the widespread adoption of movable type printing as pamphlets and entire books were printed in mass for the first time. Information was memorialized and huge libraries were created like never before in the history of humans. Ideas put to writing could be considered by countless numbers of thinkers. Eventually, learned opinions started to coalesce around a broad range of subjects. Societal opinions held for hundreds of years about certain topics started to change. These new and improved insights regarding the material world not only continued to enhance the reputation of science; certain specific Ultrathoughts tangibly improved society.

Enthusiasm for the methodology led to the overall impression that science had no limits. Any valid truth or belief can be proven by science given enough time and effort. The printing press makes it rather easy to disseminate data, so scholars, politicians, and even clergy who were confident in their truth were encouraged to share their beliefs with the ignorant masses. Certain clergy, Martin Luther in particular, believed it wise to let the public have unfiltered access to all information. He took it upon himself to translate the Christian Bible into the common German tongue.

Before this era most people never sat down and seriously considered how or why some knowledge is different than others. For many still today it is simply beyond comprehension that the scientific method itself fundamentally conflicts with spiritual beliefs. Spiritual concepts were generally hand-me-down beliefs supported by clergy and intertwined with governance. Throughout most of human history people have simply been indoctrinated into a set of beliefs, which was considered in the best interest of the person and society. God was rarely scrutinized. When and if ideas of God were held up in comparison to some foreign concept of the Godhead, it was only done by philosophers and deep thinkers. Such a thinker would contemplate in private rather than risk the ire of the masses. The public certainly didn't have access to libraries of historical data written in their own language in which to sit down and contemplate the Godhead. Leaders told people what to think, and whatever was told was in everyone's best interest.

Just as our world changed with the introduction of automated search technology, the world of the past changed with the introduction of moveable typeface. As mass-produced works became available, ideas about the workings of the body, nature, and the cosmos came under direct scrutiny by more and more people. To many it seemed the scientific method could be used to explain most anything. As enthusiasm for the scientific method grew, ideas of God himself were being reconsidered through a scientific lens. God defies all explanation, and yet the public was not enlightened about what could and couldn't be explained by science. If the distinction couldn't be clearly expressed, spiritual religions themselves might fade away.

Philosophers of the time needed to adapt and ultra-think better ideas in support of spiritual beliefs. They needed to better explain how and why physical reality wasn't all there was to the cosmos. If they failed, they would forfeit all meta beliefs; in fact, philosophy itself could fall to the religion of science. Spiritual beliefs could soon fade to irrelevance and might even falter to the point of total annihilation. There was one philosopher, the ultimate ultra-thinker, who was up to the challenge like no other.

CHAPTER 18

RENÉ DESCARTES: THE SECOND DEFENDER

Doing so in a manner similar to Thomas Aquinas three hundred years earlier, René Descartes came to rescue the spiritual from the grasp of the physical realm. Without a doubt, established spiritual religious beliefs were losing ground in the bitter battle between proofs deemed supported by the scientific method and the concepts of the spiritual supported merely by the argument of faith or tradition. Throughout the history of spiritual faith and related religious dogma, leadership struggled to define what it considered acceptable interpretations versus blasphemy. To set boundaries on the religious dogma, the church had meetings, retreats, conventions, and various councils. Over hundreds of years, participants came to settle on sanctioned beliefs that became ingrained in the practice of worship. The dogma became dense and unfaltering.

Science, being relatively new in the mind of the public, hadn't yet formed a rigid dogma. Science was adapting and evolving, and new discoveries forced change at an ever-increasing pace. The methodology of science, and indirectly the religion of science, were even daring to take on the establishment. Science sought to prove and disprove various aspects of what was previously considered truth. Much of that historical truth had been incorporated into spiritual dogma. The church, grounded by history, tradition, and precedent, could not keep pace with science. Realities of physical truths changed while church dogma stayed consistent.

Be reminded that during this period church and state were closely tied in many areas of the world. A ruling aristocracy tended to align with a specific religion, forming a theocratic style of government. If the dogma of the church was in trouble, then its partner the state was in jeopardy as well. Left unchecked, a successful challenge by science could destabilize an entire society.

René Descartes (1596–1650 CE), a French philosopher and mathematician, was a product of post-Reformation society during the scientific revolution. Being a self-described rationalist, he did not blindly accept the philosophical reflections of past philosophers; he had to figure things out for himself. While serving in the military, he had some sort of spiritual experience in which he believed a divine spirit revealed to him a new way to consider philosophy: using mathematics as a means to better understand metaphysical philosophy. He eventually became a serious Christian but had never been a church leader, and yet he ended up devoting much of his life rationalizing his spiritual faith in a manner similar to Aquinas.

To accomplish such a task, he first needed to address the uncertainty surrounding any human knowledge, be it derived from confusing aspects of the Bible or the writings of pagan masters like Cicero. He believed that all knowledge comes to us through our senses, but he looked deeper into these questions and used experimentation supported by mathematical formula to quantify knowledge. The focus of his ultra-thinking dealt with what could be gleaned from the use of scientific knowledge versus what appeared to be an innate knowledge possessed by every individual.

As was the case for Aquinas, free and open questions of this nature were particularly difficult to explore without raising the ire of the church. At the time, the church was embroiled in the Galilean controversy, since the earth-centered geocentric solar system was proving difficult to support in the face of Galileo's science and use of the telescope. Using the instrument, anyone could see that the earth moved around the sun, not the other way around.

The church, unfortunately, had spent a millennium building a tradition under the premise that the earth was the center of a cosmos that was about 6,000 years old. Earth was superior to the sun within the dogma. Leadership couldn't simply state they were wrong and that all of the historical dogma was in error. Descartes wanted no part of the Galilean controversy or anything like it. In fact, he simply abandoned some of his own work for fear of retribution.

Despite the foul mood of the church and dangerous times, he needed to quietly resolve a larger question. Could the human mind, independent of indoctrination, develop a convincing argument for the existence of God? Was knowledge of God an innate or learned skill?

As fate would have it, before he could fully consider the question of the existence of knowledge within man, he inadvertently backed into the theological discussion of the Eucharist. This odd nuance of Christian church dogma centers specifically on whether bread and wine taken at the church sacrament of Holy Communion become actual flesh and blood, or flesh and blood that tastes, smells, and looks like bread and wine. The question seemed ideal for serious scientific analysis and demanded an answer once and for all. Scientists of the era went so far as to examine partially digested bread in hopes of determining when, if, or at what point bread morphed into flesh. Transubstantiation, the metaphysical process where one matter turns into the essence of another material form, was foundational to church doctrine of the time and was presented as a literal yet inexplicable truth. Scientists accepted the challenge and decided to prove or disprove this position of the church.

Predictably, such evaluations would lead to the question of the Holy Trinity. Could a physical person, namely one Jesus of Nazareth, become a God? The church, representing the state as well, was going to end up looking foolish against the non-spiritual religion of science unless this theme was changed . . . and quickly. Descartes was the philosopher who could help the church's position, but would he dare to enter the discussion in open forum?

The philosophy of Descartes is best explained in his book *Meditations on First Philosophy* in which he develops his Ultrathoughts concerning his ideas. One of his early deductions was that a person's ability to reason is a gift from God, and therefore he would not be damned by God for using his mind to consider issues of science objectively. This general premise gave him and scientists the liberty to explore any domain of the church. Frankly, this argument sounds very much like Aquinas, but with a key difference.

For René Descartes, science and God were subject to two distinct and separate sets of rules. Explained as a kind of substance dualism, or "Cartesian dualism," he explains that all material things, including the human body, work like machines obeying laws we can test through the scientific method. However, the human mind is not material. Any application of the scientific method to that which is immaterial is logically flawed. Science is valid and may challenge as it chooses, but concepts of the meta, things like mind or God, are not subject to the rigors of science. It then follows that religious dogma is a matter of the spirit. Science cannot be applied to matters concerning God; the church can be protected to the extent it wraps itself in spiritual dogma. Descartes was an advocate of Aristotelian logic, but only within these limits. There exists a physical and a spiritual domain.

Though many view the work of Descartes as a clear and valid defense of the Christian faith, the church was not satisfied with his philosophical musings. Bear in mind, Descartes was French, and the seat of Catholic authority was in Rome. Historically Paris and Rome were rivals, and church leaders often had competing interests. From the view of the Pope of Rome, although the arguments of Descartes didn't overtly neglect the church, it certainly did not elevate the church to a position superior to that of science. The implication was that the church and state needed to stay in their lanes. Christian leadership was angry that Descartes failed to write in support of dogma directly. The published works of Descartes were banned in areas controlled by the church throughout most of his life.

Though shunned by church leadership, he wasn't executed, and his Ultrathoughts eventually gained widespread support. His position was certainly helped by the fact that his concepts tended to be in line with church reformers or modernizers. These protesters, or Protestants, mostly from regions we know today as Germany, Austria and the Netherlands, subscribed to similar but not identical Godhead designs. Regardless, most of their followers were moving toward a total separation from the design promoted by the Roman Catholic Church. The ideas of Descartes in many ways highlighted many of the same challenges pointed out by the reformers.

Protestant sects of the Christian religion tended to elevate the status of the individual believer over church leadership. In doing so, these sects walk a line of respecting the church but denying the superiority of leadership. As Descartes pointed out, people—even church people—are not the same as God. These newer spin-offs were more willing to consider the ideas of Descartes far sooner than the traditional Catholic Church.

As Cartesian dualism matured as an Ultrathought, the metaphysical issue of God in its entirety came to be considered by many Protestants as an issue that should be examined by individuals through their own mind. Be reminded that it was during this same period, again because of the printing press, that religious texts (and the Bible specifically) were being translated into various languages for the first time. Individuals were reading and meditating on concepts independently without the guide of spiritual leaders like never before in history. Reformation leaders like Jan Hus, Martin Luther, and John Calvin came to advocate for certain variations on the traditional doctrine of belief. The philosophy of Descartes acknowledges that, given the flaws of humans, people can disagree and still live in harmony with a Christian God.

Many of these newer beliefs were considered outrageous, blasphemous, atheistic, or subversive to the church and any closely tied government. These new ideas included:

- The individual is superior to the organization of the church.
- Certain historical ceremonies promoted by the church are not holy before God.
- The Christian Bible is meant to be read and contemplated directly by the individual.
- Clarification that the Kingdom of God is not here today but exists in the future.
- The church and its Pope are not infallible.
- Individuals within guidelines of spiritual texts are free to correct errors of the past.
- Physical miracles are true historically, although they are truly impossible today.

As time passed, the Catholic Church came to respect Descartes nearly as much as the Protestants. A thorough understanding of his concept of dualism came to be seen as perfectly harmonious with Christian beliefs, particularly the Trinity. To logically defend the concept of a physical body becoming a God is no mean feat, and eventually Christian church leadership would appreciate that if they embraced the idea of dualism they might be able to adequately defend any position.

In my view, Descartes presented a view in general alignment with Aquinas. While each appreciated the science of Aristotle, they stressed simple faith over logic in matters of God. Descartes, given his era, needed to be much more direct in his approach. His only logical course of action was to do as he did, specifically drawing a line between the physical and the metaphysical. Once the line became clear the church could somewhat insulate itself from the rigors of the scientific method.

This new approach, dualism, helped to resolve what were previously irreconcilable conflicts between the Godhead and science. Hopelessness, frustration, or complete cognitive dissonance had started to consume believers in the church up until Descartes. With his detailed design and descriptions of the nature of truth and fact, followers of the faith could accept certain scientific facts without feeling compelled to resolve every puzzle. A believer could, with intellectual pride, simply state that any application of science to God fails to accept the learned position of dualism. Certain things are not subject to the laws of science. By fundamentally separating reality into two realms, Descartes went back to the basics, allowing room for religion in the face of the scientific revolution.

The ideas of René Descartes pose a bit of a challenge for many today, and our interpretations of his wisdom continue to evolve. Hundreds of years ago he was viewed as an enemy of the church, yet he came to be their champion within decades. Scientists loved him as a secret champion of the religion of science, though now his Ultrathoughts are a thorn in the side of the naturalist. Descartes actually picked no side. He simply wanted to think Ultrathoughts.

Descartes was a preeminent scientist in his era and a fervent believer in Christian philosophy. His spiritual inclinations can be traced to his having visions from the divine spirit in his twenties.

Following these events, he sought to create a life with purpose. Key to his goal was to clarify his mind—to figure out a way to distinguish fact from fiction as determined by his own mind. Thinking as a left-brain oriented scientist, he used logic for his analysis. Ultimately, he determined that mathematics, more specifically analytical geometry, could be applied to concepts of philosophy. In doing so he determined that all factual truths should be connected. This very rational premise helped solidify the use of algebraic concepts in application to all science.

When many ponder this person and his Ultrathoughts today, they wonder—would he today, as a scientist, be a dogma-following naturalist? After all, he was the ultimate logical mathematician. Given the breadth of scientific knowledge and data, they're inclined to assume Descartes would certainly abandon his Christian faith. Yet we should never forget that Descartes, like most spiritual thinkers of note, was not simply a casual believer in this philosophy of God.

He had a personal experience with the spiritual realm. This is a very common characteristic of die-hard spiritual believers. Once they have this type of experience, they don't typically abandon their respect for the Godhead. The fact that he used principles of math to address philosophy is not a surprise, nor an indication of him having had a personal view that ranked the physical as superior to the meta. Rational thought, mathematics in this case, is a natural way for a left-brainer to contemplate a right-brain oriented topic. He did not come to the spirit because of his science. He used science as a tool to enlighten his spiritual self.

Cartesian dualism, this very lucid Ultrathought by Descartes, saved God from a fatal assault by science. Science and the physical realm reside in one domain and the spiritual realm in another. For this reason, though he didn't want to pick sides, he will remain the mortal enemy of the religion of science and the naturalist. Cartesian dualism accepts the spiritual realm as a fact—a fact unexplainable by the scientific method. Using our book one analogy of a carnival balloon of reality, the Cartesian concept defines a line between physical and spiritual, but this line will continue to move as more is known through the use of the scientific method. Two realms do exist.

CHAPTER 19

ULTRA-THINKING FOUR THOUSAND YEARS

In rapid succession, we've considered several philosophical Ultrathoughts concerning the nature of the Godhead and the soul spanning a period of no less than four thousand years. Up until widespread acceptance and use of the scientific method, humanity generally didn't ponder a distinction between a physical and spiritual truth. Reality itself was a blend of both. No delineation existed between physical and spiritual truth. Their view of reality was no carnival balloon in the minds of ancient people; all reality was one consideration within their mind-myth.

Godhead designs of old must be read contextually; otherwise, the reader will be misled. To understand the designer, one must understand the era. With regards to their Ultrathoughts and contemplation of what was considered allegory versus literal in the minds of human beings over the past four thousand years, I ultra-think the following:

1. The issue of literal versus meta is technically not applicable regarding the dynastic Egyptians because the society probably didn't conceptualize any hint of distinction between the physical and meta realms.

2. The early Greeks and Hellenists came to view the Godhead as potentially being more meta concept than material substance, but the society as a whole still hadn't internalized an overt distinction. The ideas of Plato and Aristotle certainly point to a distinction being made but until these

designs gained favor with the public, the public had no need to appreciate such depth of thought.

3. The first Christian philosophers circa 100 to 400 CE were challenged to form a rational theory of God that could accommodate both a material and meta presence of God. This was particularly important given their God, Jesus, transcended a physical life to become a spiritual God.

4. Circa 700 to 1300 CE—as the Christian religion matured it came to accumulate a rich set of very specific beliefs, ceremonies, and sacraments. The religion became more important than the philosophy. The religion was confusing to common folk. Church leadership was left to interpret the religion for the faithful. Believers were instructed to accept an indoctrination into approved beliefs without question.

5. As societies evolved, ideas of personal liberty spread and printed material became more available. People naturally started to question the very idea of "authorized" belief. Religion, particularly Christianity in Europe, started to be reconsidered through a scientific lens. This led to a reconsideration of its core philosophy.

6. Circa 1700 CE, largely because of the Ultrathoughts of René Descartes, metaphysical concepts were clearly permitted to be distinguished from physical truth. This allowed a philosophy of the Godhead and versions of associated religions to co-exist in a society that respected the scientific method. Society could continue to advance in a scientific world without categorically denying God.

The challenge presented by the adoption of concepts advocated by science pointed out a problem—any literal interpretation of the spiritual Godhead could be rendered moot as mind-myth came to value the scientific method more than religious dogma. Aquinas was one of the first to have to deal with this challenge, and he did so with skill. However, it was ultimately left for Descartes to offer a philosophical fortress in defense of concepts of the spiritual in his *Meditations on First Philosophy*. So far, his idea of truth, fact, and reality has offered believers the ability to maintain the logical high ground. Yet, eventually, the scientists will take this fort of spiritual solace. As society becomes more secularized, designs of the Godhead will continue to be challenged to explain how any God can be *real*. It is possible that in the near future the only unifying religion will be the non-spiritual religion of science.

Still, some of us will continue to understand the unmatched Ultrathoughts of Descartes; rationally, science won't explain all reality. Thus, the existence of a spiritual realm simply makes sense. Whether the design was that of the dynastic Egyptians, Pythagoras, Siddhartha Gautama, Aristotle, Plotinus, Muhammad, or Augustine, the Godhead seems plausible in my delusion.

CONCLUSION

B ook one, *Intentional Thought*, set forth the concept of ultra-thinking and in this book your confidence to use ultra-thinking has been built. All is now an admitted delusion or illusional truth of the mind. Though we deny no worthy science, we do appreciate that each thought of science has at its root a hypothesis. Nothing but an educated guess. If our best and brightest—our scientists—represent that truth is based on a countless number of guesses, we shall not elevate theirs above any truth created by the ultra-thinking Egyptians, Plato, Aristotle, Augustine, or René Descartes. All reality is encased in a carnival balloon of truth inflated by a willing mind.

The Egyptians incorporated some of the wildest concepts of the Godhead ever considered into their everyday society. We shall not disrespect what was quite possibly the premier society of the past three, four, or by some estimates five thousand years. Their ideas of the Godhead are bizarre to us but were worthy to them and obviously benefited all of humanity.

Greek and Hellenist thinkers built on an Egyptian foundation, bringing forth extremely lucid descriptions of the spiritual realm. Given their subject was considered during an era we today call the dawn of science, it is no wonder their views showed a flow and structure that gave clear deference to logic. "Poetic" is the best way to describe the designs of the Hellenists. Their Ultrathoughts have withstood the test of time. Many were obviously masters with few equals.

The monotheists, particularly those whose God is the One God of Abraham, put forth views that ring as truth to our Western mindset. Generally speaking, most people who seriously contemplate the Godhead today reflexively view God as one presence or substance even if they deny the worthiness of the God of Abraham. I believe the principle reason for this is the success of the Christian church in promoting its views. Most of us have been indoctrinated to conceive of the Godhead as a single God who very often takes on physical characteristics within our minds. Had the church been less successful, it is entirely possible that more people would subscribe to a different form of design.

I hope it is clear that I have no intention of slighting or disrespecting any beliefs. One day I hope to devote more time to the study of Eastern philosophy, but as of this date, I am simply too ignorant to do any discussion justice. My ultra-thinking tells me a worthy belief is that which you internalize and make part of your person. Whether one believes in God, gods, or a more vague sense of Godhead, the specifics are meaningless to anyone but the believer.

If you want a few more specifics about my views on God and several unrelated subjects of science—like the superposition of all possible states, gamma rays being cosmic erasers, aliens, and the very nature of hell—please join me in the finale.

The final book in the series is a densely packed explosion of material. The idea behind its writing is to create a catalog of several of my Ultrathoughts. Some are contentious, a few are strange, and at least a couple are downright offensive to most of Western society. With that in mind I call the third book *Forbidden Philosophy*. Book three is a bit different than one and two. Book one is a self-help book describing the concept of ultra-thinking, and this second book is a blend of history, popular philosophy, and metaphysics. I would characterize book three as my attempt to make sense of the nonsensical. Some of the views expressed may be versions of ideas you are already familiar with, and others could spur you toward your own enlightened conclusions. Regardless, I believe the book will engage your mind, and like the others, it's a quick read.

In the works is an entirely new book using the ultra-thinking premise to contemplate issues involving your financial future. My working title for the book is *Money on a Mind: A CPA Exposes the Myths of Money, Taxation, Retirement, Expatriation, Financial Predictions, and Asset Allocation.* You may have guessed that my profession lies within the realm of finance and accounting. I am currently a certified public accountant (CPA), Certified Financial Planner™, real estate agent, stockbroker, and insurance agent. I also have a Master of Business Administration degree with an emphasis in finance from a top tier university. Yes, meaningless credentials showing nothing but persistence. With that admission, I have suppressed my logical mind enough to create a few Ultrathoughts about money, the economy, and personal finance. This entirely different type of book will enlighten the reader about how their minds' impressions of financial subjects have far more to do with financial success and happiness than actual financial performance. Let's call it a fair-minded approach to managing both your mind and net worth. I ultra-think finance and economics, demoting many of my historical views in the process. I don't want to be your CPA or personal financial advisor. I simply want you to have an informed view of your own situation given the current financial *predicament* of our economy.

I naïvely started the Ultrathoughts project at the urging of my daughter roughly one year ago. What was first a casual summary of decades of notes taken soon morphed into a formal book, which expanded to three, and then a website. I continue to ultra-think obsessively about the potential of promoting the benefits of ideologically suppressed deep contemplative thought. I am excited by the idea that just maybe humanity could recognize the inherent flaw of reflexive thinking and seek to do better.

It is my vision that several, if not hundreds, of my readers will become authors who write their own books of Ultrathoughts. You are already a thinker, and I believe at this moment you are making some poetic outlines. You have made it this far and put up with my own peculiar style. You are starting to get it. Thinking is innate to our species, and our biological leaning limits our ability to think freely with an open mind. This clouds our version of the truth in a fog of bias. Passive and reflexive thinking can never escape the bias. Your currently held yet reflexive views on important subjects are less than ideal. I suggest your delusion can be improved, though certainly I shall never be a final judge of its quality. To be a thinker of Ultrathoughts one must become a fearless and purposeful thinker. Fair-minded conclusions thus derived read like poetry to the listener and truth to the author.

A true poet is not a person who seeks a quick rhythm of prose to please the party faithful, but one who challenges others to ultra-think whole-brain thoughts with intent. When you write your own, you advocate for the premise that poetry, Ultrathoughts, are worthy. If ours is a delusion then what is the harm in putting forth your thoughts to create a beautiful butterfly, all the while respecting a butterfly created by another?

You may believe I don't effectively suppress my inclination. You might believe every word I write is so filled with bias it reads as propaganda promoting the mind of a logical-left leaner. That is fine. I take no offense. The Ultrathoughts Tripartite serves more than one purpose.

The Old General I described with condescension in book one is the victim I dare not become. Should his biased theme dominate my mind-myth, the visionary I hope to be stands no chance of survival. Today I urgently seek to train a poet through ultra-thinking. If I am successful, the Old General type will never fully conquer my mind, and I shall be allowed to continue my verse.

> *"It is not enough to have a good mind;*
> *the main thing is to use it well."*
> *René Descartes*

GLOSSARY FOR FULL SERIES

collective mind (CM): Similar to *mind of society* as a societal attitude, belief, tone, style, and sensibility; a meta idea that does act with intent. Comparable to the idea of a *world soul* having a presence and/or relationship to the Godhead.

complex (dynamic) system: A system composed of many components that may interact with each other. Aggregate activity is nonlinear (not derivable from the summations of the activity of individual components), adaptive, and open. Variability is seen as an inherent property of the system although it typically exhibits a hierarchical self-organization under certain pressures.

dogma: A set of principles laid down by an authority and perpetuated by perception of dominance. A code of tenets or body of doctrine.

epigenetic: Relating to nongenetic influences on gene expression. A general term used to describe dynamics not fully understood by scientists in the field of genetics.

god/God: Superhuman presence, being, or force. Brahma, Zeus, Jesus the Christ, God of Abraham, and simply "God" are among various names used to describe a superhuman presence.

Godhead: A generalized or meta concept of God. The domain or realm of all that is godlike.

ideology: Your ideas wrapped around your personal mind-myth narrative.

indoctrination: The process of teaching someone ideas and standards with or without intent.

hard science: Often associated with the natural sciences; biology, chemistry, physics. Sciences associated with a well-defined methodological rigor.

Hellenist: A person speaking the Greek language whose outlook and way of life was significantly influenced by the Greek Empire of ancient times, regardless of heritage or geographic location.

Hellenistic era: Defined by Wikipedia.org as being from 323 BCE to 31 BCE, although dates assigned by other sources vary.

meta: Non-material, unknown, or spiritual.

metaphysical: See *meta*.

mind: Your ideas and concepts. Not quite so defined as to be a story, but similar.

mind-myth, narrative, personal story: The way you think. Your ideas woven into a metaphorical story that serves as a framework from which you perceive information.

mind of society (MOS): Societal attitude, shared beliefs, tone, style, and sensibility having no spiritual or physical presence other than the force of inertia. MOS is a meta idea that has no ability to act with intent.

monotheism: A belief in and associated worship of a specific and single God.

naturalism: see *religion of science*.

philosophy: Study and contemplation of the fundamental nature of knowledge, reality, and existence.

physical realm: The domain of reality dealing with the material substance of matter. Deals with the known or that which is deemed knowable.

polytheism: A belief in and associated worship of multiple gods.

quantum: Discrete quantity of energy. An expression used to describe a non-material presence of energy, momentum, or electric charge.

realm: Domain, area, kingdom.

religion: A belief in and associated worship of a theme, set of ideas, or controlling presence.

religion (spiritual): A belief in and associated worship of a superhuman presence.

religion (non-spiritual): Beliefs and worship that are not associated with any superhuman presence.

religion of science: A belief in and associated worship of a set of ideas that deny any superhuman presence. Naturalism or Darwinism.

science: A systematic methodology that organizes knowledge in the form of a testable hypothesis (informed guess).

scientific method: The methodology that involves observation, cognitive assumption, mathematics, and specific testing in an attempt to disprove a hypothesis.

soft science: Often associated with social sciences; economics, philosophy, sociology, psychology. Sciences ill-defined and less subject to a well-defined methodological rigor.

soul: A spiritual consideration that deals with the immaterial part of a being either human, other animal, and/or substance matter of life.

spiritual: The domain of belief, truth, or reality that deals with the immaterial, unknown, unknowable, and/or Godhead. All that is not within the physical realm.

ultra-thinking: An act of purposeful thinking in a manner that restrains personal ideology, indoctrinated belief, and existing expertise of the thinker as it forces the mind to actively seek outlandish new information.

Ultrathought: Deep contemplative thought, idea, or epiphany as a product of ultra-thinking.

world soul: A spiritual consideration that deals with the immaterial part of the cosmos, nature, universal consciousness, and self-awareness of a physical substance.